THE JUDGES OF ISRAEL

KNOW YOUR BIBLE SERIES

●●●●●●●●●●●●●●●●●●●●

A STUDY COURSE OF
THE JUDGES OF ISRAEL

●●●●●●●●●●●●●●●●●●●●

White Wing Publishing House and Press
Cleveland, Tennessee U.S.A. and Other Nations

ACD
31697

The Judges of Israel
Copyright ©2002
Published by White Wing Publishing House
P.O. Box 3000 • Cleveland, Tennessee, U.S.A. 37320-3000
(423) 559-5425 • 1-800-221-5027
http://www.wingnet.net
All rights reserved
Cover art: Sixto Ramírez
Reprint 2002

ISBN # 1-889505-39-0

CONTENTS

Important Instructions 3

Lesson One
A Broad Scope Preview 5
Lesson Two
Othniel, the First Judge 10
Lesson Three
Ehud, the Second Judge, Shamgar, the Third
Judge 14
Lesson Four
Deborah, the Fourth Judge 20
Lesson Five
Gideon, the Fifth Judge 27
Lesson Six
Abimelech, the Sixth Judge 34
Lesson Seven
Jephthah, the Ninth Judge 41
Lesson Eight
Ibzan, Elon, and Abdon, the Tenth, Eleventh
and Twelfth Judges 50
Lesson Nine
Sampson, the Thirteenth Judge 55
Lesson Ten
Eli, the Fourteenth Judge 65
Lesson Eleven
Samuel, the Fifteenth Judge, Part One 73
Lesson Twelve
Samuel, the Fifteenth Judge, Part Two 84
Examinations 96

FOR BIBLE TRAINING INSTITUTE
THE JUDGES OF ISRAEL

A Character Study Course

—Lesson One—

A BROAD-SCOPE PREVIEW

Suggested Scripture Readings: Judges 1:1 through 2:10.

Helps in Pronunciation: Flavius Josephus—FLA-vi-us jo-SEE-fus. (NOTE: In this space in each lesson, the more difficult names will be listed, with syllabic pronunciation. The syllables to be emphasized will be printed in capital letters. See the name above as an example.)

GENERAL PREVIEW:
The Old Testament *Book of Judges* deals with a rather singular period in the history of the nation of Israel. While this course will be mainly a character study of the fifteen "judges" of that period, it is obvious that their lives were shaped by the events, and vice versa. Some of the fifteen were not really "judges," in the strictest sense of the word; they were only leaders in one specific deliverance in a limited area.

This was an unique era in some ways:

(1) The nation was found to be without *one executive head*. God had not seen fit to appoint a successor to Joshua, so the government was largely tribal. Possibly God Himself desired to rule His people theocratically. At least, He would put them to a test: *Would they look to him directly in the absence of a human mediator?*

(2) The twelve tribes had been allotted their respective areas of inheritance in the Promised Land of Canaan, but in most instances they had not fully "possessed their possessions." Each tribe was to establish itself in its own territory. This

involved them in numerous conquests with the heathen peoples of the land.

(3) It was a time of succumbing to the social, political, and religious influences of the heathen populations around and among them. This, of course, brought the disfavor and anger of God upon them, along with His chastening rod.

In this introductory lesson we will give some explanation of points more or less applicable to all subsequent lessons.

CHRONOLOGY *(dates or time periods, and their consecutive order):*

There are numerous systems of chronology. Possibly Archbishop *Ussher's* system is the best known, but he lived and wrote in the 16th and 17th Centuries A.D. Continuing research and study have made this system less dependable than formerly. *Hurlbut's* system is an early 20th Century system and has been used, though not exclusively, in some of our Church publications.

Some well-researched information on chronology is found in *"The Pulpit Commentary,"* a widely read set of commentaries by H. D. M. Spence and Joseph S. Exell. Where this commentary is available to the class, or the individual student, it would be helpful to read the topic on "Chronology" in the INTRODUCTION to *The Book of Judges*.

For those who like specific dates of historical events, our main source in these lessons is the *Thompson Chain-Reference Bible*. In the reference columns, the dates are often followed by a question mark—for example, B.C. 1425 (?). This indicates that chronological systems vary, and that the date given is "probable," or "approximate." This fact must be kept in mind; variations need not cause great concern. If the individual reader's interest is great, further comparative studies may be made on his own. Depending on the system followed, the *Period of the Judges* varies from 285 to 450 years, or more: "... Somewhere between the years B.C. 1500 and 1000," according to *The Pulpit Commentary*, Introduction to Judges, page I. (See Acts 13:20.) According to the *Thompson Chain-Reference* dates, this course covers 350 years (1406 to 1056 B.C.).

Chronologists and commentators conclude that, since the judgeships were tribal, in some instances more than one judge was ruling at the same time in different parts of the possession of the twelve tribes.

DIVISIONS OF THE BOOK OF JUDGES:

Although, as stated earlier, this is a character study course, it should be of interest to look at the Bible record in three divisions:

I. *Introduction—Judges 1:1 through 2:10.* We suggest that the KEY VERSES for this division are:

"And ye shall make no league with the inhabitants of this land; ye shall throw down their altars: but ye have not obeyed my voice: why have ye done this?

"Wherefore I also said, I will not drive them out from before you; but they shall be as thorns in your sides, and their gods shall be a snare unto you" (2:2, 3).

This looks back to the latter part of *the Book of Joshua*, where Joshua was giving Israel his last charge before his death. (See Joshua 23 and 24; especially 23:1-13 and 24:1-15, 23.) He made them remember what the Lord had done. He called their attention to their situation in the land of promise. He encouraged them to continue in obedience to the law of God. Lastly, he warned them of the consequences if they allowed the heathen to remain among them.

II. *Main Body of the Book: Cycles of Oppression and Deliverance— Judges 2:11 through 16:31.* The KEY VERSES might be excerpts from 2:12-18, something as follows:

"And they forsook the Lord God of their fathers . . . and followed . . . the gods of the people that were round about them. . . . And the anger of the Lord was hot against Israel, and he delivered them into the hands of spoilers. . . . and they were greatly distressed. Nevertheless the Lord raised up judges, which delivered them. . . . And yet they would not hearken unto the judges, but they went a-whoring after other gods. . . . And when the Lord raised them up judges, then the Lord was with the judge. . . ."

As we proceed with the course, this familiar, regrettable cycle will be repeated many times.

It has been noted that the God-chosen judges were all of the "common stock." None had any reason to "glory in the flesh." But most of them were patriots or reformers—called-instruments of Jehovah, each for his times, and for the purpose of God. (See *Scofield Reference Bible:* note under Judges 2:18.)

III. *Appendix: Life in Israel during the Period—Judges 17:1 to 21:25.*

The KEY VERSE might well be 21:25—a summary of the entire period:

"In those days there was no king in Israel: every man did that which was right in his own eyes."

No particular judge is characterized in these last five chapters. The chronology is uncertain. However, the reading of this division of the book will give clearer perception of the times, making it easier to understand some of the actions of the judges.

OTHER JUDGES:

Two judges are not mentioned in the *Book of the Judges*, but they are included in our characterizations in this course. While other men were later called "judges," it seems evident that their area was limited, and that they were under the jurisdiction of a central authority. (See 1 Samuel 8:1, 2, and 2 Chronicles 19:4-7).

SOURCES OF COMMENTARY:

The Bible is our principal source book for these lessons. However, commentary helps have been gathered and incorporated from the following:

(1) *The Thompson Chain-Reference Bible—New Comprehensive Bible Helps*, by Frank Charles Thompson

(2) *Scofield Reference Bible*—notes by C. I. Scofield

(3) *Lessons in Bible Training, Volume One*—textbook used in Bible Training Institute

(4) *The Pulpit Commentary*, by H. D. M. Spence and Joseph S. Exell

(5) *Matthew Henry's Commentary*

(6) *The Zondervan Pictorial Bible Dictionary*, by Merrill C. Tenney

(7) *Bible Atlases* (Baker's and Hurlbut's)

(8) *Butler's Bible Works*, by J. Glentworth Butler, et al.—an excellent 12-volume commentary copyrighted in the late 19th Century—probably not now in print.

(9) *The Works of Flavius Josephus*—a Jewish historian who wrote in the First Century A.D., and was in the prime of life

at the time of the A.D. 70 dispersion. (Note: In this course, we are quoting Josephus more or less frequently. It must be understood that his writings, or those of any commentator, are not to be equated with the Holy Scriptures. Josephus had available to him volumes of Jewish history which could hardly be expected to have been included in the canonized Scriptures. Much of it is factually true, yet not written under divine inspiration.)

A Word About Maps: In the compilation of these lessons, numerous maps, have been checked for the locations of places mentioned in the Bible. If the class, or individual student, endeavors to use maps, it may be with some degree of frustration. It may be necessary to use two or more maps to find certain cities, rivers, mountains, etc. Name changes sometimes result in the need to do extra research. Bible maps are usually small and not easy to read. Atlas maps are some larger, but most of them seem not to have made complete entries of all places referred to in the Bible text. Despite the difficulties, it is worthwhile to use maps.

Summarily—the authors and compilers of all reference helps have put much effort into study and research. They offer their findings only in the hope that the Bible record can be more readily understood and authenticated. For the same reason, we make reference to them in this course. We repeat, however, that nothing must be allowed to take the place of the Holy Ghost-inspired Bible text.

—Lesson Two—

OTHNIEL: THE FIRST JUDGE

Suggested Scripture Readings: Judges 2:11 to 3:11; Joshua 15:13-19; 1 Chronicles 4:13.

Helps in Pronunciation: Canaanites—KA-nan-ites; Hittites—HIT-ites; Amorites—AM-or-ites; Perizzites—PER-i-zites; Hivites—HI-vites; Jebusites—JEB-u-sites; Mesopotamia—MESS-o-po-TA-mi-a; Othniel—OTH-ni-el; Kenaz—KEE-naz; Caleb—KA-leb; Kirjath-sepher—KER-jath-SEE-fer; Achsah—AK-sa; Chushan-rishathaim—KU-shan-rish-a-THA-im; Anakim—AN-a-kim; Anak—A-nak; Euphrates—U-fra-tees; Hathath—HA-thath.

THE HISTORICAL SITUATION:
As we enter the *Period of the Judges*, we find the tribes of Israel dwelling in their promised inheritance, where God had directed Joshua to locate them. The land had been taken by conquest. Under the wise leadership of Joshua, the people had been obedient, and God had wrought great victories for them. However, according to the will of God, all the inhabitants of Canaan had not been driven out immediately. Israel would need time to increase, and to properly inherit and inhabit the land. (See Exodus 23:29-33 and Deuteronomy 7:22-26.)

But they had crossed the Jordan in about 1451 B.C. Now, nearly fifty years later (about 1406 B.C.), they were still content to dwell among the worshippers of other gods. Worse yet, they had forgotten the Lord's admonition not to be ensnared by those idol gods. "And the anger of the Lord was hot against Israel" (Judges 2:20). He would leave them on their own for a season. They had been almost boastful when Joshua had tried to sober them, saying to them, "Ye cannot serve the Lord" (Joshua 24:19). "Nay; but we *will* serve the Lord," they had vowed.

Now there they were, dwelling "among the Canaanites, Hittites, and Amorites, and Perizzites, and Hivites, and Jebusites" (Judges 3:5). Their children had intermarried, and (as usual!) they were serving the gods of the heathen—"Baalim and the groves" (3:6, 7).

Then came the time for the "rude awakening." The king of Mesopotamia came against them and overcame them. This invasion was probably not expected, for they were living among a people not their own, in relative quiet. Mesopotamia lay some 400 miles east of the Jordan. Undoubtedly the hand of God had moved this foreign army into the area to serve His purpose. He would *prove* Israel (3:1, 4). Josephus, the Jewish historian, describes this *Mesopotamian Oppression* as follows:

". . . They [Israel] lost many of their soldiers in the battle, and when they were besieged, they were taken by force; nay, there were some who, out of fear, voluntarily submitted to him, and though the tribute laid upon them was more than they could bear, yet did they pay it; and underwent all sort of oppression for eight years; after which they were freed from them. . . ."

Eight years of the chastening rod were required to accomplish God's purpose. We read, "And when the children of Israel cried unto the Lord, the Lord raised up a deliverer" (3:9).

THE MAN OTHNIEL:

The deliverer was a man named Othniel. He was of the tribe of Judah. His father was Kenaz, who was Caleb's younger brother. (Remember, Caleb was one of the faithful spies sent out by Moses more than 80 years before—Numbers 13:6). Since *the Lord raised up* Othniel for this crisis, it is of interest to learn all we can about him.

He had a noble ancestry, dating from his Uncle Caleb. The tribe of Judah might be called "the apple of God's eye" among the twelve tribes, in that from this tribe would eventually proceed the promised Messiah and Saviour of the world.

Caleb, at this point in time, was the only survivor of his generation. All but he and Joshua had died in the wilderness. Now Joshua was dead also. Joshua had allotted Caleb the city of Hebron, along with "this mountain" (Joshua 14:12-15; 15:13, 14), which was inhabited by a giant people called the Anakim. Caleb and the army of Judah drove out the sons of the giant Anak (Judges 1:10).

Then an interesting episode developed, involving his nephew, Othniel. Caleb set his sights on taking the city of Debir, formerly Kirjath-sepher, some ten miles to the southwest of

Hebron. Matthew Henry suggests that this was Caleb's gesture of appreciation, to return the favor by helping the army of Judah take another city. He threw out a challenge to the younger men—"he that smiteth Kirjath-sepher, and taketh it, to him will I give Achsah my daughter to wife" (Joshua 15:16; Judges 1:11-13).

The Bible simply and briefly tells us that Othniel "took it," and that Caleb gave him Achsah as his wife.

It is hardly to be supposed that Othniel took the city without aid. Evidently he did so as the captain or general of an army. The success was probably a part of God's *raising him up*—a prelude to a greater victory at a later date.

We would not overlook the additional good fortune which came to Othniel through his wife. Apparently Caleb had given Achsah some highland ground without significant water springs on it. Seemingly she would have preferred that her new husband request "a field" of lower ground where there were more springs. Othniel's modesty may be assumed at this point. He would not press his uncle, who was now also his father-in-law, for anything more. So Achsah made the request, and Caleb gave her "the upper springs and the nether [lower] springs" (Judges 1:15).

Thus, in about 1444 B.C., God had His "deliverer" in the making for His purpose some thirty-eight years later. Now the last eight of those years had been spent under the awful *Mesopotamian Oppression*. When God at last heard Israel's cry, He had His man ready.

"And the spirit of the Lord came upon him [Othniel], and he judged Israel, and went out to war: and the Lord delivered Chushan-rishathaim king of Mesopotamia into his hand; and his hand prevailed against Chushan-rishathaim" (3:10).

God was good to Israel!

So we see the man Othniel as one who was sensitive to the moving of the Holy Ghost. This "moving" possibly began as a spirit of compassion for a people who had sinned, but had now repented. Next, his heart may have swelled with an Israelite patriotism that would not be quieted. The Spirit that was on him came on enough others so that war was waged against the mighty oppressor. The Bible gives the conclusion in few words. But Josephus, on the whole, can be trusted in his amplification of Bible events. He says of Othniel:

"... When he had procured some to assist him in this dangerous undertaking, (and few they were, who, either out of shame at their present circumstances, or out of a desire of changing them, could be prevailed on to assist him,) he first of all destroyed that garrison which Chushan had set over them; but when it was perceived that he had not failed in his first attempt, more of the people came to his assistance; so they joined battle with the Assyrians, and drove them entirely before them, and compelled them to pass over Euphrates. Hereupon Othniel, who had given much proofs of his valour, received from the multitudes authority to judge the people; and when he had ruled over them forty years, he died."

"And the land had rest forty years" (Judges 3:11).

This must have been a welcome peace, after some twenty years of careless, idolatrous living, and the oppression of a tyrannical foreign power.

One last mention is made of Othniel. He had a son named Hathath (1 Chronicles 4:13), of whom nothing more is said in Scripture.

FOR OUR ADMONITION AND LEARNING:

The apostle Paul instructs us to apply Biblical events of the past to our present life situation:

"Now all these things happened unto them [Israel] for ensamples: and they are written for our *admonition*, upon whom the ends of the world are come.

"Wherefore let him that thinketh he standeth take heed lest he fall" (1 Corinthians 10:11, 12).

"For whatsoever things were written aforetime were written for our *learning*, that we through patience and comfort of the scriptures might have hope" (Romans 15:4).

From this lesson we may be *admonished to accept admonition*. Joshua pointedly *admonished* Israel, but Israel forgot or ignored the *admonition*, thereby bringing oppression upon themselves.

We may *learn to accept learning*. Though the experience of the oppression was a good-but-dear teacher, Israel *learned* that repentance and obedience are the unrelenting requirements of God.

It is still true that if we would enjoy His favor we must embrace His truth by faith, and serve Him from the motivation of love.

—Lesson Three—

EHUD: THE SECOND JUDGE

Suggested Scripture Readings: Judges 3:12-30; Joshua 18:11-28; Judges 1:21; 20:16; 1 Chronicles 12:2.

Helps in Pronunciation: Ehud—EE-hud; Moabites—MO-ab-ites; Eglon—EGG-lon; Amalekites—AM-a-lek-ites; Ammonites—AM-on-ites; Gera—JEE-ra.

THE HISTORICAL SITUATION:

When Othniel died, Israel was again without a leader or counsellor. It was not long until they were doing "evil again in the sight of the Lord." This time God's spotlight was on the tribe of Benjamin, whose inheritance joined Judah's on the northeast, at the extreme north end of the Dead Sea, and extending westward from the Jordan.

East of the sea and extending southward lay the land of the Moabites. Moab, from whom this people sprang, was the son of Lot's older daughter, and also the son of Lot (Genesis 19:37). En route to Canaan, God had forbidden Israel to "distress" the Moabites because of Lot. But now, perhaps 125 years later, we read of a strange circumstance:

"The Lord strengthened Eglon the king of Moab against Israel, because they had done evil in the sight of the Lord" (Judges 3:12).

King Eglon solicited the assistance of the Ammonites and the Amalekites for an invasion of Israel. (NOTE: Ammon was the son of the younger daughter of Lot; also Lot's son, as we read in Genesis 19:38.) The Ammonites' territory lay to the northeast of Moab. The Amalekites were largely nomadic, but dwelt principally in the extreme southern portion of Canaan. Their origin is controversial (Genesis 14:7; 35:12; Numbers 24:20).

The Bible gives no cause for the Moabites to invade Israel. Historians differ; some suggest ambition for more territory; Josephus says the Moabites greatly despised Israel "on account of the disorders of their political government." At any rate, Israel was subdued and brought under tribute for eighteen years—years known as the *Moabite Oppression*.

Dates are conjectural here. The forty years of "rest" prior to Othniel's death would bring us to 1366 B.C.; but it is uncertain just when Israel's decline began, or when they finally called for God's deliverance. History must be given time to do its work—which records that Eglon "omitted no method whereby he might distress" Israel.

THE MAN EHUD:

Again the Bible declares that "the Lord raised them up a deliverer." This time it was Ehud, of the tribe of Benjamin. His father's name was Gera. The genealogy of Benjamin is very difficult to disentangle among the references (Genesis 46:21; Numbers 26:38-40; 1 Chronicles 7:6-12; 8:1ff). Ehud may have been a great grandson of Benjamin.

One commentator speaks of him as "a youth ... who was intrusted with the charge of carrying the tribute to the Moabite fortress ... the slight, wily, agile Israelite." Josephus characterizes him as "a man of very strong body, fit for hard labor, but *best skilled in using his left hand*, in which was his whole strength."

The Bible is more brief, interestingly pointing out his *lefthandedness*. This comes through later, however, as something more than a minor detail. Besides it being a peculiar Benjamite trait (Judges 20:14-16), it appears that Ehud was so especially equipped, since *the Lord had raised him up* as Israel's deliverer from the *Moabite Oppression*.

It may be true, as suggested above, that he was the one regularly intrusted to carry the tribute money to the house of Eglon. But Judges 3:15 to 18 clearly states that on this particular occasion he was bearing "a present," or a gift, to King Eglon from "the children of Israel." We may assume that Israel hoped in this way to cause the oppressor to look upon them more kindly than he had been during the past eighteen years.

It seems that no one else knew the secrets of Ehud's mind that day. What "the present" was, we are not told. In the inspiration of God, it is irrelevant. But it required additional carriers, for Ehud "sent away the people that bare the present," but he himself returned for a second meeting with the king.

Get the picture: Eglon dwelt in "the city of palm trees," somewhere in the area of old Jericho (Johsua 6:26)—perhaps between there and Gilgal, some five miles to the southeast (Judges 3:19). Being "a very fat man," he was sitting in his "summer parlor" where it was cool. Ehud and his assistants came, delivered the present, and left. Then Ehud returned alone on "a secret errand." One historian says Ehud told the king that he had *a dream* to impart to him, and that Eglon quickly rose to his feet in eager anticipation, thereby giving Ehud the advantage he needed. The king's servants were dismissed.

Dream or not, Ehud called it "a message from God." As soon as the king arose, Ehud thrust his dagger into him, *using his left hand*, though the dagger was on his right thigh. It was done so quickly and so unexpectedly that Eglon was caught utterly defenseless. Ehud quietly departed, closing and locking the door behind him. Evidently his composure was such that, even if his departing was observed, it created no suspicion. So Eglon lay dead without being found perhaps until evening.

Ehud used this time to rally an army. Apparently the sound of the trumpet aroused great excitement among the Israelites in all the area of Mount Ephraim and the plain near Jordan. The news of the king's death must have been both shocking and happily exciting to the Israelites. The army was probably on its way to "the city of palm trees" almost before they had time to consider that they might be totally wiped out by the Moabites.

According to Josephus, the timing was perfect. He says that when Eglon's servants found him dead, "they were in great disorder, and knew not what to do; and before the guards could be got together, the multitude of the Israelites came upon them...." Some were killed; others fled toward the land of Moab. But Ehud had not forgotten to block "the fords of Jordan toward Moab."

Although the Moabite soldiers were "all lusty [strong, robust], and all men of valour" (Judges 3:29), Ehud and his army won a total victory. Not one man of "about ten thousand" escaped!

Some commentators have called Ehud a murderer, or an assassin, then endeavor to "justify God" in helping him with the deed. Others contend that Ehud acted prematurely and wholly on his own, but that God did not bring him to account because the thinking of the times was not as it is today. They make much of the fact that no mention is made of him being made "judge," as in Othniel's case, and that it is not specifically stated that the Spirit of the Lord was upon him. It is generally assumed, however, that he judged Israel 80 years (fourscore—Judges 3:30) following the victory over the Moabites.

FOR OUR ADMONITION AND LEARNING:

Since *God raised Ehud up* for a deliverer, and since he did deliver Israel in so sweeping a victory, it seems only empty prattle to suggest a "miscarriage of justice," either on the part of the deliverer or of God Himself!

Under the law, *the death penalty* was literal. It was in the hands of the Sovereign God who is altogether *just* and *merciful.* Furthermore, Israel was *His covenant people.* It is true they had sinned against Him, but they had also "cried unto the Lord," evidently in confession and repentance.

While things were different "under grace," it remains that those who are used of God to deal with sin and Satan are often misjudged. This is part of the cross the righteous must bear.

The sacred record does not accuse Ehud. Then why should men "question God"?

SHAMGAR: THE THIRD JUDGE

Suggested Scripture Readings: Judges 3:31; Joshua 19:32-39; Judges 1:33; 5:6.

Helps in Pronunciation: Shamgar—SHAM-gar; Naphtali—NAF-ta-li; Anath—A-nath.

THE HISTORICAL SITUATION:

Very little information is available about this period of Israel's history. The chronology is uncertain. Eighty years of rest following Ehud's judgeship would advance the time too rapidly for this or the following period. We can only suppose that Shamagar's rule was sometime within those 80 years.

The area of this Philistine confrontation is not known for sure. The Philistines were generally located in the southwestern part of Canaan, along the Mediterranean Sea. However, the sparse information we have is hardly in favor of this area relative to this lesson.

THE MAN SHAMGAR:

Judges 3:31 tells us about all that is known of this man. He was the son of Anath; but who was Anath? References to Naphtali (Genesis 46:24; 1 Chronicles 7:13; Numbers 1:15; 13:14) make no mention of Anath. However, Joshua 19:38 names *Beth-anath* as one of the cities in the inheritance of the children of Naphtali. This may or may not have significance.

The name "Beth-anath" is said to mean "the temple of Anath," and the name "Anath" is said to mean "an answer to prayer." Does this suggest that Anath was so much a man of prayer that his house was known as a house of prayer, and that the city was greatly influenced thereby? If so, Shamgar's character, and his zeal for Israel, may be a reflection of his godly parentage. This is merely a thought, of course.

Commentators assume that Shamgar was of the tribe of Naphtali because of the brief references given above. The land given to Naphtali was situated in the extreme north of Canaan, adjoining the Sea of Galilee and extending north and west. This was not near the area commonly inhabited by the Philistines. Of course, it is not impossible that the 600 Philistines of Judges 3:31 were "out of bounds," or that Shamgar was out of his home territory. But, since he was a judge, he would likely have ruled in his own territory—which we only assume was Naphtali.

Even the usually affluent-speaking Josephus says only this of Shamgar: "After him [Ehud] Shamgar, the son of Anath, was elected for their governor, but he died in the first year of his government."

Shamgar is mentioned in the song Deborah and Barak sang following their victory (Judges 5:6). It is said to describe the oppressive conditions of the times—the people were afraid to travel the highways because of the Canaanite ambushments. If such was the case, Shamgar's slaying of the 600 men with an ox goad, and delivering Israel, was a greater victory than the space given to it would indicate. His valor and strength are seen in the crudeness of his weapon.

Zondervan's Bible Dictionary states that the "ox goad" was a pointed stick used to urge the yoked oxen to greater effort. It is said that Jesus referred to the goad by way of illustration when he said to Paul, on the Damascus Road, "It is hard for thee to kick against the pricks" (Acts 9:5).

FOR OUR ADMONITION AND LEARNING:

The *volume* of the material written about a person may be far less significant than *what* is written. Remember Enoch? (See Genesis 5:18-24; Hebrews 11:5; Judge 14, 15.) Then remember Methuselah (Genesis 5:21-27).

Enoch lived only 365 years and was ready to be raptured. Methuselah, Enoch's son, lived 969 years, "and he died." However, he gave the world a great patriarch—his grandson Noah.

Let us learn also from Shamgar that God can use us *if we will use what He has put in our hands*—or in our *hearts* and *minds*!

—Lesson Four—

DEBORAH: THE FOURTH JUDGE

Suggested Scripture Readings: Judges 4 and 5; Psalms 83:9, 10; Joshua 11:1-14.

Helps in Pronunciation: Deborah—DEB-or-ah; Naphtali—NAF-ta-li; Ephraim—EEF-ra-im; Zebulun—ZEB-u-lun; Kishon—KI-shon; Sisera—SIS-er-a; Issachar—IS-a-kar; Kedesh—KE-desh.

THE HISTORICAL SITUATION:
As we pointed out in Lesson One, the "Cycles of Oppression" are becoming clearly evident. The oppressions came as judgment from God upon His backsliding people.

The eighty years of rest following the rule of Ehud and Shamgar gave time for a new generation to arise. It was hard for the people to learn the lessons from history. Israel fell into sin again. They had continued to allow their possession to be inhabited by the heathen nations. They seemed not to feel the pricking of *the thorns in their sides* until those *thorns* took their advantage.

About 1316 B.C., what is known as the *Canaanite Oppression* began, and lasted twenty years. The Bible is almost silent on the description of the oppression itself. However, we can note the cunning craftiness of Satan working through his instrument, King Jabin. At the time of Joshua's conquests and the division of the land, the area pertinent to this lesson had been taken from the Canaanites and allotted to Naphtali, Asher, Zebulun, and Issachar. This area lay north and west of the Sea of Galilee.

At that time (about 1450 B.C.) and earlier King Jabin had his headquarters in the city of Hazor. When Jabin heard of the other victories of the children of Israel, he and the kings round about him mustered a great army—". . . much people, even as the sand that is upon the sea shore in multitude, with *horses* and *chariots* very many" (Joshua 11:4). But Joshua and his army, at the command of the Lord, fell upon them and won a sweeping victory. Jabin was slain, and the city of Hazor (the head of all those kingdoms—Joshua 11:10) was burned.

Now, some 135 years later, the Israelites had not *maintained* what Joshua had *attained*. Other Canaanites had infiltrated the area, possibly in mock-subjection to the Israeli tribes. Hazor had been rebuilt and was once again the seat of government for another King Jabin.

It seems a safe assumption that the Canaanites had seethed with hatred all those years since that earlier ouster of their ancestors. And the gullible, apathetic Israelites seemed not to detect "the wiles of the devil" working in the guise of an insidious "diplomacy"! Instead of maintaining their holy identity, they provoked God with their idolatry (Judges 5:8) to sell them into twenty years of oppression.

It is interesting to note that this King Jabin, like his predecessor, had many *chariots* as part of his "war machinery." In fact, it appears (Judges 4:3) that the "nine hundred chariots of iron" were what awakened the Israelites to their precarious situation. While they had been enjoying "the pleasures of sin," their "peace-loving" enemies were enjoying a "unilateral arms race"!

At the opportune moment, the "power switch" was effected; the *possessors* became the *oppressed*, right in their own land!

THE WOMAN DEBORAH:

After twenty years of *Canaanite Oppression*, the Lord heard the cries of His wayward people once again. For this time of distress He had raised up a prophetess named Deborah. So little is recorded about her ancestry that we cannot even be sure to which tribe she belonged. We are told only—

"And Deborah, a prophetess, the wife of Lapidoth [of whom nothing more is said], she judged Israel at that time.

"And she dwelt under the palm tree of Deborah between Ramah and Bethel is mount Ephraim: and the children of Israel came up to her for judgment" (Judges 4:4, 5).

The trouble brewing was in the environs of Hazor, in Naphtali. Some have assumed that Deborah was a Naphtalite, but the location of her judgment seat seems to favor Benjamin or Ephraim. Bethel was in the allotment of Benjamin (Judges 18:21, 22), and Ramah in Ephraim, perhaps six miles south. (NOTE: There was a Ramah in Naphtali, but the proximity of Bethel to Ramah favors the one in Ephraim.) As a prophetess who "judged Israel" (probably *all* Israel), it is understandable that, in a time of oppression, the people in the northern extremities might well travel the 80-to-100 miles to seek counsel.

One commentator ranks Deborah as "greatest (with Gideon) of Israel's judges." She loved the people, and they loved her; "a mother in Israel" (Judges 5:7) testifies to that. It is probable that she also was a mother of children by Lapidoth and possessed a true maternal love that extended to all those of "the chosen people," even when they did not live as they should.

Her wisdom is shown all through the planning and waging of the war against King Jabin and his allies. She was too wise to usurp authority beyond her *prophetic* unction, or that which was appropriate for a *woman* in Israel.

Some who sought her counsel may have come from Naphtali, where the oppression was the severest. They lived where they could observe the quiet implementation of arms by the Canaanites. Sensing that a surprise attack was in the making, they fled to one whom they felt could make contact with God. Apparently Deborah made that contact, then wisely sent for Barak, who was possibly the most capable general in Israel at the time. Also, he lived in Naphtali in the city of Kedesh, about twelve miles north of Hazor. He would be familiar with conditions there: the lay of the land, and the most logical strategies of war for that particular situation.

However, this well-qualified general must have been amazed at the exactness of *military detail* given him by this woman of God. Her first words to him might well have meant, to his militant mind, ATTENTION! SALUTE! *"Hath not the Lord God of Israel commanded, saying . . .?"* Then, by the power of the Spirit, she became the mounthpiece of God Himself:

"Go and draw toward mount Tabor, and take with thee ten thousand men of the children of Naphtali and the children of Zebulun.

"And I [the Lord] will draw unto thee to the river Kishon Sisera, the captain of Jabin's army, with his chariots and his multitude; and I will deliver him into thine hand" (Judges 4:6, 7).

What army general would not welcome such specific detail, and from so high a *Command*! Yet how many would pose so few questions! Barak asked only one condition. And who would dare affirm that that condition was not prompted of God? "If thou [Deborah] wilt go with me, then I will go; but if thou wilt not go with me, then I will not go" (4:8).

As though this "ultimatum" had already been divinely revealed to her, without hesitation she replied, "I will surely go with thee...." Then, as if to put the noble Barak to the ultimate test—the test both of his *humility* and his *patriotism*—she added, "Notwithstanding the journey that thou takest shall not be for *thine* honour; for the Lord shall sell Sisera into the hand of a *woman*."

Barak's nobility and his unselfish love for Israel almost leaps out to us from the pages of Holy Writ, though he spoke not a word! Personal honor? Embarrassment? Military "decorations"? Perish the thought of such senseless trivialities in the face of a nation's salvation from a jealous, vengeance-bent oppressor!

And it is true that some commentators and historians have interpreted Barak's one condition as *cowardice*, or something like "an evening of the score" with Deborah for laying upon him so dangerous a charge. But who can persist in so biased a stand after reading the whole story? A fairer and more sensible evaluation has been offered by one W. F. Alexander:

"Deborah cannot *lead* the army, but she can *inspire* it. Barak cannot *prophesy*, but he can *fight*. Thus Deborah cannot secure victory without Barak, nor Barak without Deborah. We are members one of another, and all the members have not the same office...."

It is refreshing indeed to read the full account, observing how humbly dependent the two were upon one another, yet with what straightforward boldness they filled their respective roles, step by step. And it activates our deep wells of joy to see the absolutely victorious outcome!

Back to verse 9—Deborah, we like to think, could hardly wait for Barak's silent, out-and-out acceptance of the commission, honor or no honor. Both were ready to go and set in motion the God-ordained engagement! Everything fell into place. The men of Zebulun and Naphtali responded as though something had been firing their spirits for "voluntary service."

"... He went up with ten thousand men at his feet"—or, so obedient to his orders that every one of them was eager, as it were, to put his feet in Barak's footprints! "... And Deborah went up with him"—up Mount Tabor, a perfect vantage point.

Sisera stationed his army and his much-set-by "nine hundred chariots of iron"—where? At the River Kishon! Had not the Lord said He would draw them there? The valley of the Kishon must have seemed full of Canaanite troops!

Some would have Barak growing fearful and faint-hearted at the sight, and suggest that he would have turned back had it not been for Deborah. The Bible does not warrant such an appraisal. Deborah simply said, *"Up; for this is the day . . .!"* And Barak simply *"went down from mount Tabor"* and faced the foe.

From here the story moves rapidly. "And the Lord *discomfited* Sisera . . .!" He confounded or frustrated him and his army: threw them into disorder; put them to flight! One writer says, "It was not so much the bold and unexpected charge of Barak that produced this effect, as the *supernatural* panic, a terror from God, that seized their spirits, threw them into irretrievable confusion, and made them easy prey for the sword."

From Judges 5:19-22, many commentators, including Josephus, say that God sent a rainstorm and hail, flooding the Kishon valley, blinding the enemy, and sweeping many of them away. Sisera, who had put such great trust in his *iron chariots*, left his and fled on foot!

Now, as Providence would have it, sometime earlier a Kenite man named Heber, and his wife Jael, had moved from Judah to a plain near Kedesh in Naphtali (Judges 4:11). We find in Judges 1:16 that the Kenites had gone with Judah to Canaan in Joshua's time. They were descendants of Moses' father-in-law (a Midianite) through his son Hobab, and had joined with the children of Israel in the wilderness (Numbers 10:29-33).

Heber had become friendly with King Jabin (Judges 4:17), and he and Jael were the ones who had alerted Sisera to the gathering of Barak's army on Mount Tabor. Thus far they *seemed* to be betraying Israel. But God was ordering every move.

When Sisera fled from the battle, he headed toward Kedesh. Apparently Jael and Heber's tent was on his way, so he sought hiding there. Jael welcomed him and went to extremes to make him comfortable. But when he fell asleep, she showed whose side she was on. It has been good to be friendly and at peace with the Canaanites, but when a choice had to be made, she did not hesitate. With the powerful Sisera out of the way, his armies would fall into disarray and Israel would have her opportunity to throw off the awful yoke of oppression. So she nailed his head to the ground with the tent pin!

In the slaying of Sisera, Jael had fulfilled Deborah's words to Barak. *The honor belonged to a woman.* Not to the woman Deborah, but to the Gentile woman Jael.

We need only to read chapter five (a song which Deborah and Barak sang together) to see that neither of them entertained any jealousy. While they lavished *honor* upon Jael, they gave *God* all the *glory*! Indeed, God had used them *all* by His Sovereign will and power. How fitting is the song's conclusion:

"So let all thine enemies perish, O Lord: but let them that love him be as the sun when he goeth forth in his might. . . ."

On that day King Jabin was *subdued* by Deborah, Barak and Jael; and in due time he was *destroyed* (4:23, 24).

". . . And the land had rest forty years" (5:31).

FOR OUR ADMONITION AND LEARNING:

Overall, "God's mercy endureth for ever," but He repeatedly reminds and warns us of the fact that He must withhold it temporarily when his people deliberately spurn it. His chastening hand can become painfully firm, but He always disciplines from the motive of His great love. (Read Hebrews 12:3-11.)

Concerning Deborah's and Barak's comparative anonymity, it is spiritually invigorating to observe how often the Lord uses "the common people" to do exploits while the "intelligentsia" are planning "programs" in the committee room!

We should highly respect men and women, like Barak and Deborah, who are so intent on pleasing God and edifying the body of Christ that they seem not to realize they themselves are doing anything praiseworthy.

We wonder if we often fail to give God the opportunity to "fight for us" because we have not enough faith to "go forth to battle"!

We may ask why people sometimes make moves which seem purposeless. If we will patiently wait, we may find that God knew He would need them there—a year later—ten years later. Heber and Jael probably had no idea why they "felt led" to move at least a hundred miles—away from their kindred—and, of all places, to Jabin's and Sisera's area!

Wonder what David was reminiscing about when he wrote—"Some trust in *chariots*, and some in *horses*: but we will remember *the name of the Lord our God*"! (Psalms 20:7).

—Lesson Five—

GIDEON: THE FIFTH JUDGE

Suggested Scripture Readings: Judges 6:1-8:32; Joshua 17:2 (Abiezer); Numbers 26:30 (Jeezer for Abiezer); Numbers 22:4, 7; 25:6, 16-18; 31:1-8.

Helps in Pronunciation: Keturah—Ke-TOO-rah; Abiezer—Ab-i-EE-zer; Ophrah—OFF-rah; Jerubbaal—Jer-ub-BA-al; Oreb— O-reb; Zeeb—ZEE-eb; Zebah—ZEE-bah; Zalmunna—Zal-MUN-na; Zipporah—Zi-PO-rah; ephod—EE-fod.

THE HISTORICAL SITUATION:

Chronology indicates that the forty years of rest following Deborah's judgeship ended about 1256 B.C. The *Midianite Oppression* dates from that time. However, the provocation which brought on the oppression undoubtedly began during those "rest" years.

Since the Midianites figure so prominently in this period, we will review their history briefly. Going back about 600 years (to perhaps 1853 B.C.), we find that Midian was Abraham's son by Keturah, whom he had married after Sarah's death (Genesis 25:1-7). From verse 6 we are reminded that her children were not in "the line of promise," which proceeded through Isaac.

In about 1531 B.C., Moses fled Egypt and "dwelt in the land of Midian" (Exodus 2:15), which included a large territory on the Sinai Peninsula eastward, and northward perhaps as far as the Jordan River. Jethro, the priest of Midian, put Moses over his flocks and gave him his daughter Zipporah for his wife. He dwelt there until God called him to deliver His people out of Egyptian bondage in about 1491 B.C.

Jethro paid Moses a visit in the wilderness (Exodus 18). A little later, Hobab, one of Jethro's (Raguel's) sons, was persuaded to attend the children of Israel through the wilderness (Numbers 10:29-33). (You will recall that Heber the Kenite, of the Midianites, was a descendant of Hobab, and befriended Israel in the time of Deborah and Barak.)

With the passing of time, the Midianites apparently drifted from their friendly relationship with Israel. Shortly before the end of the wilderness journey, they allied themselves with King Balak of Moab. Balak feared Israel, lest they attack his country in passing.

In Numbers, chapters 22-26 and 31, we find the Midianites becoming involved (through the Moabite alliance) in what the New Testament calls "the way of Balaam" (2 Peter 2:15), "the error of Balaam" (Jude 11), and "the doctrine of Balaam" (Revelation 2:14). (Josephus, in his *"Antiquities of the Jews,"* chapters VI and VII, elaborates on how Balaam "cast a stumblingblock before the children of Israel.")

It is possible that God's vengeance on the Midianites (Numbers 25:16-18 and 31:1-8) was kept alive in Midianite history. If so, this may account for the *"Midianite Oppression"* in Gideon's day, almost 200 years later. At any rate, "the children of Israel did evil in the sight of the Lord: and the Lord delivered them into the hand of Midian seven years" (Judges 6:1). Again, their sin was idolatry (6:10).

The oppression was great and fierce. Reading Josephus' account along with the Bible record, it appears that it began with war, the Midianites gaining the assistance of other nations until their troops were as numerous as grasshoppers. The Israelites finally fled to the mountains where they made them dens and caves in which to hide. Then the Midianites occupied the land; but at the time of harvest they would drive them out and take the fruits and grain.

Josephus says, "Indeed, there ensued a famine and a scarcity of food; upon which they betook themselves to their supplications to God, and besought Him to save them." At their cry, the Lord sent a prophet to remind them of their sin, which had brought about their pitiful circumstances (Judges 6:6-10). It was perhaps in another location that God sought out the deliverer.

THE MAN GIDEON:

The Lord's chosen vessel on this occasion was a "mighty man of valour" (Judges 6:12) named Gideon, the son of Joash. Joash was evidently the head of a portion of the tribe of Manasseh, the Abiezrites. Joshua 17:2 lists Abiezer as of that tribe. Gideon was in the city of Ophrah, threshing wheat beside a winepress to hide his activity from the Midianites, when an angel of the Lord came and sat under an oak tree nearby.

Despite the divine tenor of the angel's first words, Gideon's discouraged response (6:13) makes us wonder if he understood who his visitor was. But the angel made no mention of Israel's sins. Instead, he proceeded to lay a commission on the valorous Gideon—"Go in this thy might, and thou shalt save Israel . . .*Have not I sent thee?*" Surely it was becoming clear that this messenger was no mere man!

Humble man that he was, Gideon reasoned that he was unqualified in just about every way. But he was met with an assuring promise: "Surely I will be with thee, and thou shalt smite the Midianites as one man."

Gideon was more interested now. This was no small promise. Perhaps he visualized the "grasshoppers for multitude" horde of Midianites, and realized that only God Himself could smite them merely "as one man" by means of a down-trodden, brow-beaten, hunger-ridden people such as Israel was after seven years of almost total oppression! But who was he to lead his people to such a victory? He needed a sign from heaven; not because God was not great enough, but because he deemed himself so small. He needed a sign—not because he doubted God, but to confirm that this was of God! And God gave him the confirmation "by fire."

When the angel had turned Gideon's "present" (6:18) into an "offering" (v. 19), it was consumed by supernatural fire! Now Gideon was so sure he had seen God's face that he feared death! But he would live to carry out his calling! And there was no time to be lost. That same night he must do a thing that would provoke the Midianites to come together "as one man" to be slaughtered!

The throwing down of the altar of Baal, the cutting down of the grove, the building of an altar to God, and the offering of a burnt-sacrifice did the work! When morning came, all was astir! Who had done this? And soon the word was out! First, the Baal-worshipping Israelites demanded that Joash bring his son forth to be killed.

Was it God who moved Joash to make a *right-about-face*? If Baal were god, he could plead his own cause. Instead of letting

Gideon be slain, he gave him a second name: *Jerubbaal*—meaning "let Baal plead." In other words, if Baal were god, let him destroy his opponent if he could! Rather than dropping dead at the hand of a false god, "the Spirit of the Lord came upon Gideon, and he blew a trumpet; and Abiezer [the Abiezrites] was gathered after him" (6:34)!

From that moment on, it was GOD every step of the way. *Gideon's* messengers went through Manasseh, Asher, Zebulon, and Naphtali, and GOD brought his army together. *Gideon* laid the fleece before the Lord, and GOD gave the double-confirmation (6:36-40). That second morning *Gideon* was up early to check on the fleece, but GOD was up first! There lay the dry fleece with dew all around it!

Gideon's army pitched at Harod in the Plain of Esdraelon, with the Midianites to their north. But although the Lord had moved in the gathering of Israel's troops, He used the large response to teach His people a great lesson: That God does not depend on *numbers*; He uses *dedicated men*.

The story is well known about the reduction of Gideon's army. The "fearful and afraid" numbered 22,000, leaving 10,000. But for God's purpose, this was still too many; so He commanded *Gideon* to bring the 10,000 down to the water (probably the well, or spring, of Harod), but GOD would administer the test—*"I will try them for thee there"* (7:4).

Attitude would figure heavily in this final diminution. God told Gideon to observe each soldier closely. Those who lapped water as a dog would lap with its tongue were to be set apart. These probably maintained an attitude of watchfulness, alertness, and readiness, lest the enemy should be waiting to catch them off guard. They probably remained on their feet, cupping the water in their hands and lapping it hastily. Those who bowed on their knees to drink were also set aside. They probably put their faces in the water, drinking in a careless, self-satisfying attitude, thinking more of the thirsty flesh than of Israel's deliverance.

When the last man had drunk, it seems that God was interested only in a count of the smaller group—a mere 300! These were the watchful, ready-for-battle "lappers."

"And the Lord said unto Gideon, By the three hundred men that lapped will I save you, and deliver the Midianites into thine hand . . ." (7:7).

We must not forget that our study is about *Gideon*. We may be prone to observe the *army*, but God was also proving its *captain*. We read not a word of resistance or argument. Gideon was *in command*, but he was even more *under command*. Whatever the Lord said, Gideon did. No matter how unlike military strategy, no matter how unsophisticated, no matter how "unorthodox" the orders, *the man Gideon* obeyed.

Now God has a way of encouraging and strengthening those who stand ready to do His will. Gideon was due an added lift at this point. He was a brave leader—God knew that. But He knew also that he was flesh. We can imagine this valiant, God-fearing warrior crying out in silent, inward fear and trembling, as David did later on—"...*He knoweth our frame; He remembereth that we are dust*" (Psalms 103:14)! So God strengthened his heart and hand, and fortified his spirit and soul!

He caused an insignificant, unnamed Midianite to have a dream of seeing a cake of barley bread coming tumbling into the host of Midian, smiting and flattening a tent. Gideon and his servant were sent by night to the tent of this very man, at the exact moment when he would be relating his disturbing dream to a fellow-soldier.

If Gideon feared being discovered, he kept it to himself. And if, when they reached the enemy camp, he inwardly fainted at the sight of the "grasshopper-like" multitude literally filling the valley, he only gripped the Unseen Hand more firmly! If the tempter laughed in his face, bringing to his mind "the pitiful three hundred" who would engage this "sand of the sea side" host that very night, he only took a still firmer grip and stayed to *"hear what they say"* (7:11).

The interpretation of the dream was what Gideon needed to hear, for it revealed that this mighty army actually feared Israel—"This is nothing save the sword of Gideon... for into his hand hath God delivered Midian, and all the host" (7:14).

Gideon stayed to worship! Only then did he return to his own camp to make ready for the attack. He lost no time. God's chosen "minority" was quickly given the simple orders. Gideon gave each one a *trumpet* (Josephus says they were rams' horns), an *empty pitcher*, and *a lamp* (maybe a pine torch). Nothing is said about swords and spears. If they carried such in their scabbards, they were secondary weapons in *God's fight*!

It becomes clearer now why God had culled out the fearful and the careless. He would use only the few who would *take orders* and *act in unity*. "Look on me, and do likewise," commanded Gideon. He would go with one group of one hundred. All eyes and ears were to be turned and tuned in his direction. When he would blow his trumpet, all would blow their trumpets, shouting, "THE SWORD OF THE LORD, AND OF GIDEON!" When Gideon would break his pitcher, all would do likewise, exposing the lamps to the view of the enemy.

They approached "the outside of the camp in the beginning of the middle watch," perhaps about 10 o'clock, the middle watch of three being from ten until two. Suddenly one trumpet blast, and the shout! Then 300 more joined in! Next, the night sky seemed full of lights all around the Midianite camp!

Confusion broke out! Swords came into play—*Midianite against Midianite!* The host fled, but Gideon's 300 "stood every man in his place"—on the Lord's side! They had nothing to fear. As the enemy "ran, and cried, and fled" toward the Jordan, Gideon sent messengers to alert the 31,700 "reserves." These endeavored to block all passages of the river, but some 15,000 escaped (8:10).

The men of Ephraim, who had not been summoned by Gideon, joined in the fight and beheaded two Midianite "princes," Oreb and Zeeb, bringing their heads to Gideon. These Ephraimites contended with Gideon for not including them. Gideon's good spirit is seen in his wisdom on that occasion. He gave them credit for a greater accomplishment than his own. Their anger quickly cooled when they saw that they were sufficiently recognized.

Then Gideon and his 300 crossed the Jordan in pursuit of the Midianites who had escaped, especially Zebah and Zalmunna, two kings of Midian. The men were faint from lack of food, so Gideon asked bread of the men of Succoth and Penuel, cities in the inheritance of Gad on the east side of Jordan. These unappreciative "brethren" refused to give them aid. Gideon declared that he would punish them after he had taken Zebah and Zalmunna. The 15,000 escapees were with those two kings—all that was left of Midian's army of 135,000. The slain up to this time numbered 120,000.

Briefly concluding, Zebah and Zalmunna were captured and eventually slain. The inhabitants of Succoth and Penuel were properly chastized, and Gideon returned home. Israel showed their gratitude by requesting that he become their judge, and after him, his son and his grandson. Gideon accepted the judgeship, specifying however that God would, in fact, be the ruler (8:23).

A sad note: Gideon collected the gold jewelry and other ornaments taken as spoils from the Midianites. With it he made an *ephod*. (See Exodus 28:4-14; a sacred priestly vestment representing God's presence when His will was being sought, under the system of the Law.) Gideon's intentions may have been good, but they seem not to have been inspired of God. He was not a Levite, and had no priestly unction. Some presume that he did not use the ephod himself; but he eventually allowed its use to be abused (8:27). We must remember, however, that his name is among the faithful "cloud of witnesses" in Hebrews 11:32.

Gideon had 70 sons, and he had a forty-year rule of quietness, or peace. Then he was succeeded by one of his sons.

FOR OUR ADMONITION AND LEARNING:

When we lose sight of our God-given privileges of the past, we stand to lose out on present blessings. The Midianites' relationship to Israel through Moses was lost along the way. Though God used them to chasten His own people, they were destroyed in the very process of being used!

Israel never fell so low that God would not hear them when they repented and prayed to Him. Even at this present time, though the Jews are undergoing their longest dispersion, the time seems near when *they will look upon Him whom they have pierced*, and He will be merciful once more. And backsliders from the truth of the gospel must be made aware of the longsuffering of God and His compassion on those who show godly sorrow.

If God should need a "300-minority" in the Church today, would **I** be in the number? Would **you**? And, with all of our intellectual and theological "progress," what would be our *attitude* should God strip us of it all and send us forth "armed" with rams'-horn trumpets, empty pitchers, and pine-knot lamps?

—Lesson Six—

ABIMELECH: THE SIXTH JUDGE

Suggested Scripture Readings: Judges 8:33-35; 9:1-57. Concerning Shechem, see Genesis 12:6, 7; 33:18, 19; 37:12-14; Acts 7:15, 16 (Sychem); Joshua 24:32; 20:7; 1 Kings 12:25; John 4:5-8 (Sychar?).

Helps in Pronunciation: Abimelech—a BIM-a-lek; Shechem—SHEE-kem; Baalim—BA-a-lim; Baal-berith—BA-al-BEE-rith; Gerizim—GER-i-zim; Thebez—THEE-bez; Issachar—IZ-a-kar; Shamir—SHA-mer; Jair—JA-er; Gilead—GIL-e-ad.

THE HISTORICAL SITUATION:
The situation in this period (about 1209 B.C. to 1206 B.C.) was unlike the previous ones, in the main. However, it was the same in that "the children of Israel turned again" (Judges 8:33) unto idolatry. This time they were not oppressed by another nation. They were not calling to God for help. And the "judge" was in no sense like those who had preceded him for the past 200 years.

It appears that a decidedly apathetic attitude had developed during the forty years of "quietness" after the defeat of the Midianites. Gideon had had no desire to be Israel's judge (8:23). The people's worship of the ephod may indicate a slack hand; not that he meant to be undutiful, but that he had laid the responsibility on the people to look to God, when he had said, "... *the Lord shall rule over you.*" He may have instilled this same attitude in his seventy legitimate sons, since none of them seemed to aspire unto leadership upon their father's death.

It was only a step from making a god of their own ephod to going "a whoring after Baalim"—the same idol system their fathers had fallen into between the death of Joshua and the judgeship of Othniel (Judges 2:10-13; 3:5-7). "Baalim" is the plural word for Baal, and *Baal-berith* means "the god of covenants." Since Israel was a covenant people, the subtilty of Satan may have used "berith" as a cunning, deceptive substitute in their minds. It seems incredible that they should have become so utterly *forgetful* and so *conscience-seared*, but the word of truth declares:

"And the children of Israel *remembered not* the Lord their God, who had delivered them out of the hands of all their enemies on every side:

"Neither shewed they kindness to the house of Jerubbaal, namely, Gideon, according to all the goodness which he had shewed unto Israel" (Judges 8: 34, 35).

When Gideon died, it was as though Israel gave a sigh of relief that the one last restraining influence was out of their way. "... As soon as Gideon was dead ... the children of Israel turned again...."

THE MAN ABIMELECH:

He was hardly a "man" in principle; but he was every whit "man" as a depraved son of Adam.

Abimelech was a son of Gideon by a concubine, whom Josephus names Drumah. Her family lived at Shechem, a city which historians variously place in Manasseh and Ephraim. Judges 17:2 lists it in the inheritance of Manasseh when Joshua divided the land; but 1 Chronicles 7:28 lists it in Ephraim. We may assume that Abimelech's mother was of the tribe of Manasseh, as Gideon was, and that she lived at Ophrah, about 30 miles north of Shechem, at least until Gideon died.

The prominence of Shechem in Israel's history, and the fact that his mother's people were Shechemites, probably worked together in favor of a scheme which Abimelech may have been turning over in his mind for some time. At any rate, after Gideon's death, Abimelech went to Shechem and "communed with" his mother's brothers, and also with her father (9:1). This "communication" resulted in a sort of political-race "kick-off," with his grandfather and his uncles all "campaigning" for him.

The men of Shechem were inclined to "give him their vote," because he was a fellow-Shechemite. They gave him "campaign funds" from the Baal-berith treasury, with which he "bought" men's support—"vain and light persons, which followed him" (9:4).

The imaginations of his evil heart are seen in his slaying of his seventy "brethren, the sons of Jerubbaal." (They were his half-brothers.) There is nothing on record to indicate that any of them had the least desire to rule. He may have reasoned that the launching of his campaign might result in a challenger; so he removed that threat before it developed.

Despite this despicable act of treachery, the Shechemites "made Abimelech king." And Israel as a whole remained so apathetic as to raise no voice against his evil deeds! (Apparently they accepted his leadership, for it is said that he "reigned three years over Israel"—*all Israel*, supposedly.)

But the big "acceptance rally" was somewhat blighted by a voice from the top of nearby Mount Gerizim! Jotham, one son of Gideon, had hidden himself, escaping the execution that befell his brothers. God prophesied through him by the use of a parable (9:7-20). (Some prefer to call it a "fable," because of the inanimate figures employed—trees, vine, and bramble.)

The parable was rich, both in noble, beautiful allegory, and that which was far from beautiful. It may be summarized as follows:

God had capable and worthy men who could have ruled Israel honorably, but they were unwilling to leave "the good life" and subject themselves to the rigors of public or sacred office, even though a whole nation would be blessed through their God-given wisdom and ability. By their refusal to serve, they were virtually inviting the useless, fruitless, corrupt and hurtful character to "Come thou, and reign over us" (9:14).

Jotham shamed them for their ungratefulness toward his father and his father's house by allowing the horrible slaughter without remonstration. With a touch of "holy sarcasm," he told them that they and Abimelech should loyally rejoice in one another, if indeed they had "dealt truly and sincerely with Jerubbaal and his house" by what they had done. If not, they should expect their action to backfire!

Then, between verses 21 and 22, there are three years of silence, as the record goes. Jotham's words may have been eating them like a canker, but there is no hint of repentance. So God sent an evil spirit, and the very men who had put Abimelech in office turned his own treachery on him. It was an effort to clear themselves of involvement in the shedding of innocent blood, making Abimelech bear the full blame.

So infamous a character is undeserving of "equal time" with the nobler ones, so we will be somewhat brief. A man named Gaal—possibly a Canaanite—got in the arena, as it were. He sided with the Shechemites against Abimelech. His self-ambitious oratory was music to their ears. "Would to God this people were under my hand!" (9:29). Abimelech had been rejected, but was hardly out of the way!

Gaal challenged him to fight it out. Then Zebul, Abimelech's confidant, alerted Abimelech, and at the same time deceived Gaal by pretending to aid him. Zebul detained Gaal at a strategic point until Abimelech's army clearly had the advantage. Then he bared his deceit and dared Gaal to go forth to fight. Treachery was running rampant!

Abimelech won an overwhelming victory. He took the city of Shechem, and salted the ground to render it unproductive. The few Shechemites who escaped fled to a tower, and Abimelech and his men gathered boughs of trees, put them in the hold of the tower, and set them on fire, burning to death about a thousand men and women.

Intoxicated by his apparent success, he went to Thebez, some ten miles northwest of Shechem, to take it also. In terror, the people all fled to a strong tower. Abimelech besieged the tower and was about to burn it. *But his time ran out!* Once again God used a woman—anonymous to us, but known to Him—to cast a piece of millstone down upon Abimelech's head, breaking his skull.

All but dead, yet full of vain pride, he ordered his armorbearer to slay him with the sword, "that men say not of me, A woman slew him" (9:54). The young man obeyed the tyrant's last order. God had rendered unto Abimelech his just dues. The evil men of Shechem had reaped their awful harvest. *"...And upon them came the curse of Jotham the son of Jerubbaal."*

Has not God said, "Vengeance is mine; I will repay, saith the Lord" (Romans 12:19; Deuteronomy 32:35)?

TOLA: THE SEVENTH JUDGE

THE HISTORICAL SITUATION:

Little can be said except that conditions remained relatively quiet in Israel as a whole. Abimelech's presumptuous rule was short. It is possible that this period overlapped some of the quiet years of Gideon's time. However, it is reckoned that Tola's judgeship lasted twenty-three years, beginning about 1206 B.C. Issachar lay just north of Manasseh, but Mount Ephraim (actually a mountain range) was in the inheritance of Ephraim on the south of Manasseh. Shamir was a city in that area.

THE MAN TOLA:

Only two verses are given to this evidently good and capable man. His father's name was Puah, and his grandfather's name was Dodo. The names Tola and Puah seem to have been old family names, carried by sons of the original Issachar, son of Jacob. (See Genesis 46:13; Numbers 26:23; and 1 Chronicles 7:1.) Though Tola was of the tribe of Issachar, it seems clear that he was judge over all Israel, and that Shamir, his seat of government, was more centrally located in Ephraim.

Undoubtedly the turmoil caused by Abimelech had left the nation very much disquieted and unrestful. Tola "arose to defend Israel" at that time. We are not told if actual attacks were made by enemy nations. Possibly his method of defense was of a preventative nature. Matthew Henry's suggestion seems reasonable:

"... God animated this good man to appear for the reforming of the abuses, the putting down of idolatry, the appeasing of tumults, and the healing of the wounds given to the state by Abimelech's usurpation. Thus he saved them from themselves, and guarded them against their enemies...."

He ruled twenty-three years, evidently until his death.

JAIR: THE EIGHTH JUDGE

THE HISTORICAL SITUATION:

Conditions seem not to have changed, but the location of governmental functions did. Historically, Gilead was a region on the east side of the Jordan which Moses gave to the half tribe of Manasseh almost 270 years before the time of this lesson, in about 1183 B.C. (See Lesson Seven for more concerning Gilead.) We note that there were thirty cities in the area, collectively called Havoth-gilead—meaning "the villages of Gilead." (See Numbers 32:40, 41.) Camon (9:5) was a city about 12 miles east of the Jordan River in upper Gilead. It may have been Jair's seat of government.

THE MAN JAIR:

Jair was a Gileadite, of the tribe of Manasseh. He, like Tola, was the namesake of an earlier ancestor. The fact that he judged Israel twenty-two years, apparently until his death, speaks well of him as a man of peace and of satisfactory judgment. We cannot know, however, whether or not the apostasy seen in Judges 10:6 was working during Jair's rule.

The limited information about the man himself forbids much conjecture. The fact that "he had thirty sons that rode on thirty ass colts, and they had thirty cities" in Gilead seems irrelevant. However, Josephus mentions that Jair's sons were of good character, good riders, and that their father entrusted them with the government of their respective cities. Another commentator suggests that these colt-riding, "knightly sons" show that Jair himself was a princely man.

FOR OUR ADMONITION AND LEARNING:

In Romans 8:7, 8, Paul tells us that ". . . the carnal mind is enmity against God: for it is not subject to the law of God, neither indeed can be. So then they that are in the flesh cannot please God." The flesh, left unrestrained by government and discipline, has a natural bent to backslide. Israel—in the days of *"every man did that which was right in his own eyes"*—admonishes us by ensample never to give the flesh advantage.

Theocracy is not compatible with "politics" as a method of establishing leadership. Abimelech may be thought of as "a corrupt politician." Since the people were worshipping Baalim at that time, we should not be surprised that so many were apathetic about the atrocities in which he engaged himself. A "lukewarm" church tends to wink at sin and to tolerate false teaching, often thinking that material prosperity is a sure evidence of God's favor. The Laodicean church's reproof should set this misleading idea straight.

The account of Israel's "bramble" judge should remind us that qualified men and women who refuse theocratic appointments can be to blame for many of the reverses which the Church suffers. Ambitious, conniving men find their opportunity when God-anointed men excuse themselves of responsibility.

There is an old adage which says, *"Give an unscrupulous man enough rope and he will hang himself."* It is true that wrongdoing brings its own downfall eventually. The tragedy is that so many innocent people are influenced and corrupted by the evil ensample before he comes to the rope's end. Israel gave Abimelech the rope, thereby making themselves as irresponsible as he was. The damage done was irreparable. May the Church be admonished!

It is said that Tola and Jair did nothing "memorable" during their reigns. That could be passing "unjust judgment" on the "judges." Do God's instruments have to be "celebrities" in order for their work to be deemed important? Is not this a "worldly" practice? Paul shows us what the Church's attitude should be:

". . . Those members of the body, which *seem* to be more feeble, are necessary:

"And those members of the body, which *we think* to be less honourable, upon these we bestow more abundant honour; and our uncomely parts have more abundant comeliness" (1 Corinthians 12:22, 23).

How many pancreases have you *seen*? None? Yet we would quickly die of diabetes without the pancreas!

How many "livers" have you seen outwardly giving "that winning smile," or deftly performing the meticulous work of the hands? None? Yet, in its "out-of-sight" position it performs at least four functions necessary to the health and life of the body!

The Lord sets each member in the body of Christ as He pleases. It just could be that those He has set "out of sight" are keeping the flambouyant, crowd-swaying ones "alive"!

—Lesson Seven—

JEPHTHAH: THE NINTH JUDGE

Suggested Scripture Readings: Judges 10:6-18; Judges 11:1 to 12:7; Numbers 26:28-30; 1 Chronicles 7:14, 17; Romans 3:9-18 (Psalms 14:1-3 and 36:1-4).

Helps in Pronunciation: Jephthah—JEF-tha; Ashtaroth—ASH-ta-roth; Mizpeh—MIZ-pa.

THE HISTORICAL SITUATION:

In forty-five years (1206 B.C. to 1161 B.C.), Israel had made *full cycle* again in their pattern of periodic repentance and backsliding. And once more their sin was *idolatry*. No matter how great God's deliverances, they could forget Him and forsake Him almost overnight!

The expression "that year," or about 1161 B.C. (Judges 10:8), seems to say that the return to evil practices took place rapidly, possibly within the first year after the death of Jair. They must have been secretly lusting after other gods for some time, but had restrained themselves lest their good judge should reprove them or be grieved with them. If such were their case, they should have had an even greater fear of, or respect for, the true God. But, as David and Paul have said, *there was no fear of God in them* (Romans 3:9-18; Psalms 36:1-4).

This time, all restraint was thrown to the wind and they left out no god—*except the Lord, the only true God* (10:6)! Earlier generations had served Baalim; now Ashtaroth, another plurality of gods, was added. Then, whatever idols were served by the neighboring nations, or the peoples they had allowed to continue living in their allotted inheritances, Israel served those also.

The anger of the Lord was commensurate with the degree of Israel's sin. They had gone deeper into idolatry than ever before, and God's anger was "hot against Israel, and he *sold* them into the hands of the Philistines, and into the hands of the children of Ammon" (10:7). Commentator A. C. Henry gives the following exposition on the clause "He *sold* them":

"A forcible expression, implying the handing over of the people into the hands of their enemies, as if God had no more any property in them or concern about them; as if He said, 'Ye are not my people, and I am not your God;' and as if He said to the heathen, 'Take them, and do as you will with them; they are yours, not mine' (Leviticus 26:14-39; Deuteronomy 28:15-68)."

It has been said, "This time the punishment was as signal as the crime. Two nations at once attacked Israel on the west and on the east—the Philistines and the children of Ammon." However, the eastern part is known in history as the *Ammonite Oppression.*

The oppression by the Ammonites began in the land of Gilead on the east side of Jordan, then spread to the west into the tribes of Judah, Benjamin, and Ephraim. *"Israel* was sore distressed" (10:9) indicates that *all Israel* was under Ammonite and Philistine occupation and oppression.

After eighteen years, in about 1143 B.C., God's "hot" anger finally made them cry out to Him in confession—*"We have sinned against thee . . . . "* And their sin was twofold: (1) They had forsaken God, and (2) they had served Baalim. It has ever been true, "No man can serve two masters . . . " (Matthew 6:24).

But this time *confession alone* would not satisfy God. He was nauseated at their repeated "foxhole promises"! Reviewing His many deliverances and their continued pattern of forsaking Him, He said, *"Wherefore I will deliver you no more"!* Then He advised them to seek help from the gods they had been *serving* and let them provide deliverance.

The people knew they deserved this rebuff. They acknowledged they were due some punishment, and they were ready to suffer it if only God would deliver them from their oppressors in the end. And they finally came to the place where there were no more favors that they could ask; there must be some *doing* of what they had known all along they must do. "And they *put away the strange gods* from among them, and *served the Lord. . . . "*

Only at this point of reformation and restitution was the Lord "grieved for the misery of Israel." True, they had suffered much at the hands of their enemies. No doubt the eighteen years of physical and mental anguish had been exceedingly great. But now that they had seen their sin, they were totally *miserable* in their soul-depravity. *Disciplinary punishment* they could bear at the hand of a merciful God, but they felt they would die if the torture of their sinful condition were not relieved!

The compassion and empathy of Almighty God cannot resist the cry of godly sorrow and sincere repentance. He would answer their prayers just as they had offered them; not in immediate, unconditional deliverance, but by "whatsoever seemeth good" (10:15). They would have to face their enemies, this time in the name of the one Lord God. He would give them a deliverer from among themselves, but they would have to seek him out, then submit to his leadership. It was not going to be easy.

THE MAN JEPHTHAH:

Jephthah was a Gileadite. The Gileadites were of the half tribe of Manasseh, on the east side of Jordan; but in the course of time, they had settled also in the inheritance of Gad. Some historians hold that there was never a particular man named Gilead; but certain Scripture references seem to refute this stand. Statements such as 'Gilead begat Jephthah," and "Gilead's wife bear him sons," are difficult to understand other than that Gilead was a proper name of a father of children. (See also Numbers 26:28-30 and 1 Chronicles 7:14, 17.) If the time element seems a problem, we have already found that it was common for there to be namesakes in later generations.

We assume, from the Bible record, that Jephthah was the son of Gilead by an unnamed harlot, possibly before he took a wife (Judges 11:1). When Gilead's legitimate sons were old enough to think for themselves, they rejected Jephthah as a brother (half-brother) because he was "the son of a strange woman." It is true that the ceremonial law had forbidden that an illegitimate son should "enter into the congregation of the Lord" (Deuteronomy 23:2), in view of the required purity of the "holy nation." However, it is doubtful that *purity* was the motive in the minds of Gilead's sons.

The rejection, apparently, was during the time when the nation of Israel was almost wholly given over to idolatry, much of their "worship" involving the most lewd immorality.

It is more likely that *covetousness* was their motive; their *inheritance* would be greater if Jephthah did not share in it. Some have suggested that they were ashamed of him; but again, did Israel know shame at that time? They may, of course, have used that as an excuse.

At any rate, we get the first glimpse of Jephthah's character in the face of his being disowned. He offered no resistance. He gave their motive the benefit of the doubt. If his father was still living, Jephthah made no appeal to him. He simply "fled from his brethren . . . " (11:3). He may have considered that they would resort to dangerous measures if he stayed among them. He went and "dwelt in the land of Tob," which *Baker's Atlas* locates "on the fringes of civilization . . .possibly in the east-Jordan area." *Zondervan's Bible Dictionary* is more specific—"a fertile district in Syria, extending northeast from Gilead." (See 2 Samuel 10:6, 8—"Ish-tob," in Syria.)

Those who choose to think the worst of Jephthah make much of the statement, "there were gathered *vain men* to Jephthah, and went out with him" (11:3). They brand him as a "freebooter"—a plunderer, or pirate. This is only biased assumption, of course.

Matthew Henry writes more kindly of him: "Being driven out by his brethren, his great soul would not suffer him either to dig or beg, but by his sword he must live; and being soon noted for his bravery, those who were reduced to such straits [the unemployed], and animated by such a spirit, enlisted themselves under him . . . . "

With Jephthah as their captain, they became an army, probably coming to the aid of any who needed assistance in a just cause. Undoubtedly it was in this way that he became known as "a mighty man of valour." (Consider David's case in 1 Samuel 22:1, 2.)

Evidently Jephthah and his army were becoming *valorous* while Israel was suffering the *Ammonite Oppression* for eighteen years. The overall account of his life would lead us to reason that he was being *prepared of the Lord*. Otherwise, how do we account for his thorough knowledge of Israel's earlier history, as he relates it in Judges 11:12-27? How do we account for the utter incapability of all but him to lead Israel's defense against the oppressors? How do we account for the sudden humility of his brethren? Surely it was all God's doing!

When Israel had finally humbled themselves and gained the Lord's compassion, He set the stage for the final scene of the oppression-drama. He caused the Ammonite army to gather and encamp in Gilead (10:17). Israel could plainly see that the enemy intended no longer merely to oppress them, but to drive them out or destroy them. The Ammonites had not counted them friends or allies merely because Israel had worshipped their gods. Now that they had repented and returned to the service of the living God, they could not with good conscience surrender their God-given inheritance without resistance.

So Israel assembled an army and encamped in Mizpeh, some fifteen miles east of the Jordan in south-central Gilead. Their problem was that they had no leader; no captain or general. *But God had one for them.* However, in this case it would enhance their already humbled condition to lay upon them the burden of making the selection.

The situation was desperate. Time was wasting. Two armies would not continue to face each other for very long without one advancing. Perhaps the offer of an *award* would produce a volunteer for leadership. But none came forth, even when the award was the promise, "... He shall be head over all the inhabitants of Gilead" (10:18).

Who but God Himself inspired the next move? "... The elders of Gilead went to fetch Jephthah out of the land of Tob" (11:5). It was either swallow their pride or die. If they offered Jephthah an apology, it missed the record. We can hardly find fault with him for subjecting them to something of an "inquisition." Were they merely hoping to exploit him for their own ends? Would they *send him back to Tob* as soon as the hoped-for victory was won? He must have a committal from them.

"Did ye not hate me, and expel me out of my father's house? and why are ye come unto me now when ye are in distress" (11:7)?

Their response seems somewhat "feeble," but perhaps their embarrassment made clarity difficult: "Therefore we turn again to thee now, that thou mayest go with us, and fight against the children of Ammon...." At least they were being honest; but up to that point it was very much a one-sided proposition.

As Jephthah waited, perhaps he could not hide the hurt and the disdain at their unapologetic attitude. But they had withheld the promise of award until the last: "... And be our head over all the inhabitants of Gilead."

It was out at last—and perhaps it was something of a "clearing of the air" for all concerned. But Jephthah must be sure. Had he misunderstood? "If ye bring me home again to fight against the children of Ammon, and the Lord deliver them before me, shall I be your head?"

He was assured that he had understood correctly, God being their witness. So, without further hesitation, he went with them. Despite the tenseness at first, we like to think there was a lightness of heart which may not have been fully concealed. The illegitimate "boy-become-man," once expelled for no fault of his own, was "going home"! The longing of his lonely heart had let it slip—"If ye bring me *home* again...." Perhaps in his fondest dreams he had never dared think it would ever be! But now, if he were not slain in battle, the enjoyments of "home" would be his!

At Mizpeh, where his army was already encamped, he "uttered all his words before the Lord" (11:11). We are left in hallowed secrecy as to the unburdening of his heart. Maybe he gave praise to God for the unknown way in which He had led him those many years; for the family reconciliation; that at last his valor could be used in the service of his nation—and God's; and that he would be privileged to lead, or judge, the people (if God spared his life), who would need much teaching and guidance after so many years of apostasy and oppression.

Jephthah was not "sword happy." He made a sincere effort to "negotiate" peace. The Ammonite king tried to make a "boundary dispute" of an event that had happened some 300 years before in Moses' day (Judges 11:12-28). Jephthah knew history, and he relayed it by messengers; but the king paid him no heed. It was evident that the border lines were not the real issue in the Ammonite king's mind. He thought Israel had been beaten down so low by the oppression that they would either give up without a fight or be easily overcome if it came to war.

But one thing this heathen king had no knowledge or understanding of—*"Then the Spirit of the Lord came upon Jephthah..."* (11:29). Immediately he moved his army to the point of confrontation.

Those who would be his critics must, at this point, concede that this was God's hand-picked man of the hour. Some, however, fail to acknowledge this, hastening on to the well-known incident of his vow to God—which has been called "rash," "unadvised," "barbarous," or "egotistical."

The hoped-for success of the battle weighed heavily upon this general in whom Israel had placed such great confidence. He was God's man, but he was flesh. His zeal for God soared high. Nothing seemed too good to offer God if He would "without fail deliver the children of Ammon" into his hands. So great a *plea* deserved a great *offering:*

". . . Whatsoever cometh forth of the doors of my house to meet me, when I return in peace . . . shall surely be the Lord's, and I will offer it up for a burnt offering" (11:31).

The battle was fought, and the victory was overwhelming; so great that "the children of Ammon were subdued before the children of Israel." But for Jephthah, the joy of the victory was short-lived! The news had reached his home ahead of him, and his daughter, his only child, was the first to meet him in joyous celebration! At the sight of her, his vow to God loomed up before him. In the sudden agony of grief, he rent his clothes, telling her of his vow!

Consider the man Jephthah very soberly at this point. He might have cursed God, who could well have had a sacrificial beast first on the scene. He could have cursed God for allowing him to make the vow. Instead, his devotion to, and fear of God was greater than his love for the only child he ever hoped to have! "I have opened my mouth unto the Lord, and I cannot go back."

The kind of father he was is proven by the daughter's reaction of love: "My father, if thou hast opened thy mouth unto the Lord, do to me according to that which has proceeded out of thy mouth; forasmuch as the Lord hath taken vengeance for thee of thine enemies . . . " (11:36).

Did Jephthah offer his daughter as a burnt-offering? This has been the subject of endless controversy. Some appeal to Leviticus 20:1-5, and hold that such a man as Jephthah would not violate the law of God against human sacrifices. (Molech-worship included the offering of children.) Leviticus 27:1-8 is thought by some to have been the solution to Jephthah's problem: If vows involved *persons,* they could be redeemed with money.

Those who insist that Jephthah redeemed her, point to the young woman's appeal to *bewail her virginity,* and the conclusion that *she knew no man.* They point to the strong desire of all Hebrew women to be mothers, and claim that she and her father agreed that she would remain a virgin all her life as the "redemption price"—perhaps in lieu of a money-redemption. It appears, however, that this would have made her both the *offerer* and the *sacrifice.* But it is argued, since she was an only child, Jephthah's part in the sacrifice would have been that there would never be an issue to carry on his family name.

The greater weight of opinion is that Jephthah actually offered her as a burnt-offering. (Josephus says he did.) It is reasoned that he did not understand the money-redemption provision of the law; or that, in the awful dilemma, he concluded that it was better to offer up his only child than to break his vow to God, who had known about it from the start. The greatest appeal to this view is the statement that he *"did with her according to his vow which he had vowed . . . ."*

That "the daughters of Israel went yearly to lament" her has raised the question: Did they lament her *death* or her *virginity?*

If the offering was made, did God accept it? Perhaps another question will provide the answer: Would God, through the Holy Ghost, have inspired the writers of Holy Scripture to include Jephthah in the role of a great man of faith (Hebrews 11:32) if he had been a murderer?

After this, Jephthah won another victory over the contending Ephraimites who falsely accused him of slighting them (Judges 12:1-6). His wisdom in that instance reminds us of the simple but great wisdom of Solomon in the instance of the two mothers who claimed the same child (1 Kings 3:16-28).

Jephthah died when he had judged Israel six years (about 1143-1137 B.C.). Some think his sorrow over his daughter greatly shortened his life. Of course, we cannot be sure of this.

FOR OUR ADMONITION AND LEARNING:

How is it that men will multiply their gods, yet ignore just one—the only true God? The fallen nature is prone to go any way but Godward. We are reminded by Israel's chastisement to thank God for the Cross of Christ and the sanctifying blood.

The oppression of sin can be lifted only by the route of godly sorrow, repentance, and turning to God with the whole heart. Repentance must manifest itself in consistent conduct. God is not mocked. He knows when we mean it.

We often hear of "diamonds in the rough." Jephthah was one. No one could see beyond the blot of his family background. When the multitudes of Israel, the chosen line, could not produce one qualified leader because of the prevailing ungodliness among them, the once-despised outcast was brought forth, "polished" by the hand of God. Surely Israel must have felt reproved!

Jephthah's vow stands as a warning against a fanatic zeal that is not according to the knowledge of God's rightly divided Word of truth. Vows are not to be despised. When once made, they should be kept. "When thou vowest a vow unto God, defer not to pay it; for he hath no pleasure in fools: pay that which thou hast vowed" (Ecclesiastes 5:4). Jephthah did this, in one way or another. But as a rule, if the purpose of the heart is fixed on God, a vow will not be required to prove it.

—Lesson Eight—

IBZAN, ELON, AND ABDON: THE TENTH, ELEVENTH, AND TWELFTH JUDGES

Suggested Scripture Readings: Judges 12:8-15; Joshua 19:15 (Bethlehem in Zebulun).

Helps in Pronunciation: Ibzan—IB-zan; Elon—EE-lon; Abdon—AB-don; Aijalon—AJ-a-lon; Hillel—HILL-el; Pirathon— PEER-a-thon; Amalekites—AM-a-lek-ites.

THE HISTORICAL SITUATION:

This period in the rule of the Judges, beginning about 1137 B.C., was markedly uneventful so far as noteworthy happenings go. One writer has called it "the calm after the storm," referring back to the years of the *Ammonite Oppression* and the throwing off of the yoke through Jephthah's victory. Also, the "storm" may have included the tragic outcome of Jephthah's vow, which was revived in the minds of the people every year by the lamentation over his unfortunate daughter.

Now there was peace and quiet. Domestic interests such as home and family life were given more attention. Israel was in that part of the cycle where the Lord was their God. This is seen in the fact that they had judges in peaceful times, and not just when they needed a deliverer.

But the history of Israel declares that they could not live uprightly very long when life became easy. They would grow careless and vain. They seemed never to know when the nations around them were plotting to exploit them. First they would become unduly trustful of the heathen peoples; then they would mingle too freely with them; and eventually they would begin serving their idol gods.

Whether or not the other nations understood Israel's gullibility, it is certain that Satan knew it! He worked his evil designs through the various peoples who were under his power. We have already seen that when Israel was not in enemy hands, they were getting ready to fall there. Later on, David summarized them accurately when he said:

50

"When he [the Lord] slew them, then they sought him: and they returned and enquired early after God.

"And they remembered that he was their rock, and the high God their redeemer.

"Nevertheless they did flatter him with their mouth, and they lied unto him with their tongues.

"For their heart was not right with him, neither were they stedfast in his covenant" (Psalms 78:34-37).

We need only to read the first verse of the next chapter (Judges 13:1) to see that this period of apparent peace was actually plagued by a deceitful undercurrent of lust to return to idols. But the three judges under study in this lesson may have done their best to teach and guide the people aright.

The chronology of these three judgeships is not certain. Since the three were from different tribes of Israel, the periods may be overlapped to some extent, beginning as stated earlier, about 1137 B.C.

With a total of only eight verses of Scripture being given to the three, even with the help of history it is difficult to know if we are overplaying or underplaying the importance of their administrations.

THE MAN IBZAN:

Commentators are of little help to us on the ancestry of Ibzan. First, there were two Bethlehems: the well-known one in Judah where later Christ was born, and another in Zebulun (Joshua 19:15), said to have stood about seven miles northwest of Nazareth. Since the three verses about Ibzan do not mention the tribe, we are not sure if he was from Judah or Zebulun.

Both Josephus and Matthew Henry place him in Bethlehem of Judah; and they are probably right. However, some think he was from Zebulun because of the statement in Judges 12:11, "And after him, Elon, a Zebulonite . . . . " Had it been of great importance, no doubt the record would have made it clear.

The personal interest which Ibzan took in the marriages of his sixty children seems to characterize him as a loving and caring father. The significance of the word "abroad" is uncertain. It can hardly be supposed that he sent his sons among other nations to find themselves wives, or that he brought in foreign young men to be husbands to his daughters. It seems more reasonable that he simply brought his children up virtuously, then at the proper ages for each one to seek a companion, he trusted them to remember his teaching and to choose wisely.

Apparently his seven years as judge were the last years of his life. It has been suggested that he was made judge at this late date on the basis of his wisdom as a father, which was probably known far and wide.

THE MAN ELON:

Peace continued to prevail. Israel did well in seeing that Ibzan should have a successor. Past experience had taught them the value and the necessity of having a governing head in authority at all times.

That Elon *lived, judged,* and *died* is hardly a glamorous record. But it was far better to have nothing spectacular to show for his ten years in office than to leave behind him a three-year file of atrocities, as did Abimelech. We should not be surprised if heaven reveals many good testimonies from those who were blessed by Elon's reign.

THE MAN ABDON:

Abdon was of the tribe of Ephraim, the city of Pirathon being there. He was the son of a man named Hillel. Matthew Henry calls attention to Abdon's rule in these words:

"... In him that illustrious tribe begins to recover its reputation, having not afforded any person of note since Joshua; for Abimelech the Shechemite was rather a scandal to it...."

We will recall that "the men of Ephraim" had shown a cantankerous, jealous spirit both in Gideon's day (Judges 8:1-3) and in Jephthah's (Judges 12:1-6). Now they had a man of peace from their tribe as Israel's judge for eight years.

Like Jair's colt-riding sons, Abdon's "forty sons and thirty nephews ... rode on threescore and ten ass colts." (NOTE: The Hebrew for "nephews" is "sons' sons," or grandsons.) It seems that they were either judges and officers, or well-bred gentlemen, and that Abdon also was a man of distinction.

By the end of his reign, which was probably also the end of his life, the makings of another Israelite apostasy must have been looming on the horizon. Perhaps he was spared the sorrow of sensing his people's drift away from God. On the other hand, could it have been that he contributed to it simply by doing nothing?

The statement that he was buried "in Pirathon in the land of Ephraim *in the mount of the Amalekites"* may have no pertinent meaning. But it does call to mind that the Amalekites had a long history as enemies of Israel.

The original Amalek was a grandson of Esau (Genesis 36:12). The Amalekites were the first to launch an offensive against Israel in their journey through the wilderness (Exodus 17:8-16). While their principal location was in the extreme south of Canaan, they had at some time penetrated the area now allotted to the tribe of Ephraim, considerably north and west of the Dead Sea. (Further references may be of interest: Numbers 14:41-45; Judges 3:13; Judges 6:3, 33; 1 Samuel 15:1-9.)

FOR OUR ADMONITION AND LEARNING:

Peace and safety are more greatly appreciated immediately after periods of danger and distress. Regrettably, the long duration of quiet prosperity so often results in God's blessings being taken for granted. The devil is a wily foe. He uses the abundance of material things to blind and numb the people of God to spiritual deficiencies. This time in the *Period of the Judges* may have lulled Israel into a sort of stupor which the Philistines found to their advantage in the time of Samson.

There are none so weak and helpless as those who were once Christians, then begin to put their trust in temporal things and their own devices. When the enemy makes his attack, they seem more defenseless than those who never knew God!

It is admirable for any man—monarch or pauper—to give his best to the training of his children. Ibzan's sons and daughters apparently appreciated their father's wise and loving concern that they all should establish stable and happy homes. This speaks well for the virtue of a two-way, open relationship between parent and child.

There are those who would gladly surrender the accumulated wealth of a lifetime for a record like Elon's. Their "mark in the world" has turned sour. They are well known, but wish they were not. How much better it would be just to be at peace with themselves and with God, than to have their great collection of the laurels and badges of the worldly celebrity!

It is highly probable that, when the books are opened in heaven (or wherever), there will be those eligible for rich rewards whose earthly file contains not one note of commendation for their unassuming deeds of love and kindness.

On the other hand, there are those who can ride with Abdon and his seventy, yet keep their priorities straight and their hands and garments clean. There is no plane of life on which we cannot be witnesses to others on the same plane—if we only will!

—Lesson Nine—

SAMSON: THE THIRTEENTH JUDGE

Suggested Scripture Readings: Judges 13-16; Joshua 19:40, 41 (Zorah and Eshtaol); Numbers 6 (Nazarites).

Helps in Pronunciation: Eshtaol—ESH-ta-ol; Nazarite—NAZ-a-rite; Timnath—TIM-nath; Ebenezer—EB-en-EEZ-er; Delilah—de-LI-la; Sorek—SO-rek; Etam—EE-tam; Manoah—ma-NO-ah; Aphek—A-fek.

THE HISTORICAL SITUATION:

We must return to Judges 10:1-7, then link it with Judges 13:1, for the overall view of this *Second Philistine Oppression* of Israel. Scripture briefly introduces two oppressors—the Philistines and the Ammonites—then proceeds to pursue the second-mentioned first. The *Ammonite Oppression* was of shorter duration—eighteen years (1161 to 1143 B.C.). The *Philistine Oppression* would last forty years (1160 to 1120 B.C., approximately).

It is written that *"the children of Israel* did evil in the sight of the Lord," and that "the anger of the Lord was hot *against Israel."* Then, "that year" (about 1161 B.C.) "they"—the Philistines and the Ammonites—began the oppression (Judges 10:6-8). But in the middle of verse eight, the eighteen-year domination from "the other side Jordan" is taken up and followed to its conclusion under Jephthah. This was in the inheritance of Manasseh, but it spread into Judah, Benjamin, and Ephraim (10:9).

The Philistines dwelt principally in the southwestern part of Canaan, along the Mediterranean Sea and inland. The inheritance of Dan lay in the southern area of Philistine territory. (NOTE: A second Danite area was located in the extreme north of Canaan. See Judges 18. Bear in mind that Judges 17 through 21 are not to be reckoned chronologically with the first sixteen chapters.) The events related in Samson's day covered a limited area in the southern Dan and Judah.

Since *all Israel* had been "sold into the hands" of their enemies, it will be seen in later lessons that other areas also were being oppressed during this same period of time.

THE MAN SAMSON:

Samson is one of the few whose recorded history dates from before his birth. His father, Manoah, was a Danite who lived at Zorah, a city near the border of Judah. His mother, whose name is not given, was barren, but "the angel of the Lord" promised them a son. She was warned not to drink wine nor strong drink, and to eat nothing unclean until the child was born.

"For, lo, thou shalt conceive, and bear a son; and no razor shall come on his head: for the child shall be a Nazarite unto God from the womb: and he shall *begin* to deliver Israel out of the hand of the Philistines" (Judges 13:5).

"Nazarite" meant a person who was separated wholly unto the Lord, and especially dedicated to God. The person might take the Nazarite vow himself, which was the usual thing; or, rarely, as in Samson's case, he might be declared a Nazarite by the Lord. Usually the vow was for only a short period; but it varied at the will of the one taking it. For Samson (as apparently for John the Baptist later on—Luke 1:15), it was for life.

God gave Moses the regulating laws for Nazarites (Number 6). They were very exacting, but three articles were especially prominent: (1) Total abstinence from strong drink, and anything made of the grape; (2) letting the locks of the head grow, with no razor coming upon them; and (3) keeping clear of any pollution from a dead body.

That God Himself should declare Samson a Nazarite would indicate that the "separation" was to have a special significance to Him. This must be taken into consideration when we are prone to criticize Samson's actions. He was a specially prepared instrument by whom God would *begin to deliver Israel* from the cruel oppressor. (Consider Romans 9:14-24 in this context.)

Manoah was greatly concerned about the angel's announcement to his wife. Heavenly visitations are indeed matters for concern. Since Manoah had not been present, he was perplexed. Was this a man of earth, being used of God—something like a prophet? Or was he truly a heavenly personality? The visitation was so unusual, and his message so awesome, that Manoah felt impelled to seek further understanding of it. This child was to be *his* son also, and he must share the responsibility of rearing him. So he "intreated the Lord," or earnestly pled that He should send "the man of God . . . again" (13:8).

God answered his prayer, and Manoah was convinced of the visitor's heavenly nature when he "ascended in the flame of the altar" (13:20). Like Gideon, he feared that he and his wife would die because they had "seen God." But his wife's faith brought the calm of assurance that God would take care of the whole situation.

The story of Samson's childhood is brief:

"And the woman bare a son, and called his name Samson: and the child grew, and the Lord blessed him.

"And the Spirit of the Lord began to move him at times in the camp of Dan between Zorah and Eshtaol" (Judges 13:24, 25).

We suppose this moving of the Spirit was something more than some indication that he was an "exceptional child" intellectually. It was probably a showing of great physical strength, in strange and unusual ways, beyond what was reasonable for a child. God would direct men's attention onto this instrument of deliverance before the time. Perhaps it would make his actions easier to accept later on.

Samson was born probably about 1160 B.C. Since he judged Israel twenty years, then died in about 1120 B.C., his judgeship must have begun in about 1140 B.C. The record does not state specifically when he was made judge, but it was probably following the slaying of the thousand Philistines (Judges 15), after which it is said, "And he judged Israel in the days of the Philistines twenty years" (verse 20).

If the above calculation is accurate, then he was probably only a late-teenager during the events of Chapter 14. He had gone down to Timnath, apparently a Philistine city some ten miles southwest of Zorah. There he fell in love with one of "the daughters of the Philistines."

As the custom was in those days, he asked his parents (actually his father) to arrange with the young woman's parents for the marriage. Of course, his father and mother objected. How could it be that their divinely appointed son, a Nazarite, should think of marrying among the "uncircumcized Philistines"?

Samson's real character began to come to light at that point. He simply said, "Get her for me; for she pleaseth me well." Those parents were probably very heavy-hearted, thinking that their obstinate son was frustrating all of God's plans for his life.

"But his father and his mother new not that it was of the Lord, that he [the Lord] sought an occasion against the Philistines: for at that time the Philistines had dominion over Israel."

Israel was in a state of resigned submission to their oppressors. We are told that there had been any national repentance, though it is clear that there was a remnant who still feared God and prayed to Him. In this state of resignation, God Himself initiated "an occasion against the Philistines." In other words, there would have to be an *agitator* in Israel to give the Philistines some opposition. Samson was *God's agitator!*

(In this train of thought it is noteworthy that the oppressors became very active about this same time in another area—Ebenezer and Aphek, to the north and east of Samson's "theater of action." See 1 Samuel 4. It does not seem unreasonable that Samson's agitation could have sparked the Philistine activity in that area.)

As we read the story of this marriage and the seven-day marriage feast, we must bear in mind that the Lord was directing "in mysterious ways, His wonders to perform." The slaying of the lion led to the beehive carcase, evidently over a considerable lapse of time. The carcase full of honey led to the riddle, with the anticipation of award to the winner. The riddle led to the artful deception which turned into a villainous threat on the bride's life. The discovery of the deception *agitated the agitator,* who, by the Spirit of the Lord, slew the thirty men to obtain garments to settle the matter of awards.

The bride's betrayal (to save herself and her father's house from being burned) resulted in a temporary separation when the bridegroom went home to Zorah without her. And the separation laid the ground for the next agitation. If it all seems "juvenile" or petulant, we must not discount the fact that "the Spirit of the Lord" was furnishing the inspiration and the strength. We are reminded that "Out of the mouth of babes and sucklings hast thou [the Lord] ordained strength because of thine enemies, that thou mightest still the enemy and the avenger" (Psalms 8:2).

We must be mindful that the events of Samson's activites cover a period of more than twenty years; therefore we do not know how much time passed between these events. *"But it came to pass within a while after"* the riddle episode that Samson's anger cooled sufficiently for him to think of a reconciliation with his wife. He went down to Timnath, but her father would not let him see her, explaining, "I verily thought that thou hadst utterly hated her; therefore I gave her to thy companion: is not her younger sister fairer than she? take her, I pray thee, instead of her" (15:2).

Matthew Henry offers a logical observation concerning Samson's reaction to the above incident. He suggests that Samson took his father-in-law's action as an affront to the whole nation of Israel, rather than to him personally; and that he did it on behalf of the whole nation of the Philistines. In other words, it was a public assault, so he would react with a public assault.

It was the time of harvest, so he caught 300 foxes, tied firebrands to their tails, and let them loose in the grain fields, the vineyards, and the olive orchards. In this way, the vengeance would be felt, through impoverishment, by thousands of Israel's oppressors.

When it was learned that "the son-in-law of the Timnite" woman had done this, the Philistines, evidently afraid of the strong-man Samson, laid the blame on the woman and her father for agitating the agitator again. So they burned the two with fire. But Samson still claimed the woman as his wife, so their shifting the blame away from him onto her only made him more angry. He threatened further vengeance, and carried it out by open warfare—"he smote them hip and thigh with a great slaughter" (15:8). It is supposed that he rallied some Israelites to help him.

Following this slaughter, Samson went to a rock called Etam, probably to watch and see what the Philistines' next move would be. Etam was in Judah, and the people of Judah were troubled when the Philistines followed Samson, encamping at a place called Lehi. When they learned that the Philistines were aiming to catch and bind Samson, they evidently presumed there would be trouble in their land.

They blamed Samson for disturbing their "peace of oppression," and 3,000 of the men of Judah went to the rock to bind him themselves and deliver him to the enemy. Samson wouldn't resist his *brethren,* but he asked them to promise that they would not kill him themselves. They agreed.

So they bound him and delivered him to the Philistines. And again God moved. When Samson approached the enemies' camp at Lehi, they shouted as if to gloat in the fact that he was in their hands at last; delivered by his own people. But while the shouting continued, "the Spirit of the Lord came mightily upon him, and the cords that were upon his arms became as flax that was burnt with fire, and his bands loosed from off his hands" (15:14).

As God had ordered, a new jawbone of an ass lay nearby. Before the jubilant Philistines realized he was loosed, he was laying them low with the jawbone, God directing every swing of his arm! Soon one thousand of his attackers lay dead, and apparently, what the hordes of the remaining Philistines did was not worth putting in the sacred record!

"And Samson said, *With the jawbone of an ass, heaps upon heaps, with the jawbone of an ass have I slain a thousand men.*"

Josephus interprets these words as words of vain pride; that Samson claimed the credit for his strength instead of glorifying God. He attributes the following thirst to God's chastisement. He has the conqueror begging God for water, and confessing to God, who finally shows him mercy.

Matthew Henry's "tribute" seems more appropriate:

"Samson was celebrating his own victory, since the men of Judah would not do even that for him. He composed a short song, which he sang to himself, for the daughters of Israel did not meet him, as afterwards they did Saul, to sing, with more reason, *Samson hath slain his thousands....* He did not vaingloriously carry the bone about with him for a show, but threw it away when he had done with it...."

Consider this: If he sang the words, he sang them "in the Spirit" that was still upon him. If he merely spoke them, he did so under the unction of God!

Whatever *Judah* did—whether or not they repented of the wrong they had done to their brother—it appears that *Israel* may have honored him with the judgeship following that occasion.

The *Thompson Chain-Reference Bible* leaves a twenty-year time lapse between chapters 15 and 16. This would assume that Samson's twenty years as judge were relatively peaceful. However, from the chronology in 1 Samuel, chapters 4, 5, and 6, there was much Philistine activity going on elsewhere.

Perhaps it was God who deemed that His agitator should go into action once more. So we see Samson going to Gaza, not far from the seacoast, and involving himself with a harlot. He was recognized by the Philistines, and a plot was laid to kill him in the morning. The Gazites laid wait all night in the gate of the city, but somehow Samson was made aware of their ambush. Josephus relates his escape as follows:

"... Samson, who was acquainted with their contrivance against him, arose about midnight, and ran by force upon the gates, with their posts and beams ... and carried them away on his shoulders, and bare them to the mountain that is over Hebron, and there laid them down."

The Philistines were reminded that the strong man who served Israel's God was still very much alive, and with undiminished strength!

Sometime after this, Samson once again fell in love with another Philistine woman. Her name was Delilah, and she lived in the valley of Sorek, probably not far from Zorah. By now, the Philistines understood that their only hope of conquering Samson was to discover the secret of his great strength, then contrive some means of divesting him of it. In Delilah they saw their opportunity, probably knowing her character better than did Samson.

It is said that there were five 'lords of the Philistines." They engaged Delilah, for a price, to get the secret from him; and she turned all her capricious deception on him. Somewhat playfully for a time, he matched her caprice with his own artful wit (Judges 16:7-14).

According to his own suggestions, she bound him (1) with seven green withs, (2) with new ropes, and (3) with the seven locks of his Nazarite hair being woven into the warp and woof of a weaver's beam. But each time he freed himself as if his bonds were nothing!

Delilah then began to put his love for her to the test. The 1,100 pieces of silver must be hers! So "she pressed him daily with her words" —if he loved her, he would bare his heart and soul to her! *And at last he did!*

61

He explained to her the Nazarite vow, and told her that if his head were shaved, he would become *weak* and would be *like any other man.*

Delilah could almost feel the silver in her hands! She called for the lords of the Philistines and assured them that the secret was out. They gave her the coveted silver. Then, while Samson slept with his head in her lap, she had a man to shave off his seven locks. She then awakened him with words he had heard three times before: "The Philistines be upon thee, Samson."

Surely this Nazarite would have sensed immediately that his hair was gone. But he would "run the bluff" as long as he could. If the Lord were pleased to help him, he would not lose face before his betrayer. So he concluded that he would "go through the motions" of *shaking himself.* If he could feel that his strength was not the same, he still did not know that *the Lord Himself* had departed from him. If the *Lord* were still there, perhaps He would save him in some other way.

But no; he found himself alone—*weak, and like any other man!* His own words must have stabbed him like a dagger! What a sad commentary!

"But the Philistines took him, and put out his eyes . . . and bound him with fetters of brass; and he did grind in the prison house" (16:21).

The strong man had sinned, in that he had trifled with the one thing that had kept him in the favor of God until now: he had carelessly defiled the holy vow—the sacred covenant that God Himself had initiated!

But God was not through with Samson. God never forgets His covenants. As for Samson, he must have been full of regrets. Remorse must have burned his soul like fire! His *sight* was gone, but he could *hear* his captors celebrating and praising their gods for their great victory. But all he could do was wait to see what the Lord would do.

As his hair grew again, the Lord remembered His vow. The time passed, and the Philistines continued their celebrations. In God's time, they gathered in great numbers. The house was full, including all of their lords. There were even 3,000 upon the roof. Samson was called in to make them sport—possibly as a jester. Unfortunately for them, they situated him "between the pillars" (16:25)—"the two middle pillars upon which the house stood, and on which it was borne up" (verse 29).

This poor, blind Nazarite asked a seemingly small favor of the innocent lad who attended him. In their merriment, God caused the multitudes to place no significance on Samson's feeling of the pillars. From the main floor to the roof-galleries, all minds were on Samson's "sport." They could not know that he was also praying.

"O Lord God, remember me, I pray thee, and strengthen me, I pray thee, only this once, O God, that I may be at once avenged of the Philistines for my two eyes."

Taking hold of the pillars, he continued: *"Let me die with the Philistines."* And God answered him—every word! The house fell upon the lords, and upon all the people therein, as Samson pulled down the supporting pillars! "So the dead which he slew at his death were more than they which he slew in his life."

The funeral scene (verse 31) concludes the biography of this man who had judged Israel twenty years. Though his sin found him out, he was *the instrument of God's vengeance,* though it often seemed his own. We cannot argue with the faithful roster—"... Samson ... out of weakness ... made strong" (Hebrews 11:32, 34).

FOR OUR ADMONITION AND LEARNING:

Men are prone to judge one another; and there is a place for such judgment. But we must stand instructed by the One who will be our Judge in the end: "Judge not according to the appearance, but judge righteous judgment" (John 7:24). Like Samson, the man we judge so freely may be an instrument of God's vengeance.

When we take undue liberties with God's holy covenant, we quickly find that God is no respecter of persons!

When we lay our heads in the lap of SIN, we may expect to awake in the hands of SATAN! He "shaves" us of our power with God while we sleep!

Let us beware of our own claims! We are not "Samsons" with special privileges and powers merely because we *think so highly of ourselves.* Though we all may be "born to serve the Lord," as the song goes, do you know of more than one Samson in Scripture?

When our "brethren" collaborate with the enemy against us, pleading "peace at any price," just stay "in the top of the rock Etam," and give God time to give you strength to overcome.

Some may have "learned" how to "shake themselves," making others think they still have the Lord with them. But in the final analysis, the "shaking" in inconsequential. The question is: *Are they shaking down any fruit from the tree?* The all-wise Master had declared, " . . . The *tree* is known by his *fruit*" (Matthew 12:33).

—Lesson Ten—

ELI: THE FOURTEENTH JUDGE

Suggested Scripture Readings: 1 Samuel 1:9, 12-17, 25; 1 Samuel 2:11-17, 22-25, 27-36; 1 Samuel 3:9, 16-18; 1 Samuel 4:1-18; 1 Kings 2:26, 27.

Helps in Pronunciation: Hophni—HOF-ni; Phinehas—FIN-e-as; Shiloh—SHI-lo; Elkanah—el-KAN-a; Belial—BEE-li-el; Zadok—ZA-dok; Ichabod—Ik-a-bod.

THE HISTORICAL SITUATION:

The chronology of the early years of Eli's judgeship (according to 1 Samuel 1), begins in about 1171 B.C. Reviewing our studies of other judges, this would fall sometime during Jair's reign in Gilead on the east of Jordan, and about ten years before Jephthah's short reign. However, he must have been judge since about 1181 B.C., since he had judged Israel forty years (1 Samuel 4:18) when he died about 1141 B.C. He was ninety-eight years old at death (4:15); therefore he may have been in the *priestly* office many years before he was made *judge*.

Apparently, the conditions which brought on the *Ammonite* and *Second Philistine Oppressions* still existed at that time. In fact, if the chronological calculation is dependable, the *Philistine Oppression* was at its hottest, but in another locale. This takes up the thread of history where we left it in the *Book of the Judges*. The Philistine are still formidable enemies, though in Eli's realm the first thirty years seems quiet (1171 to 1141 B.C.). It appears that there was a degeneration in morals, and therefore a loss of the favor of God, after Eli's sons became priests.

Eli lived at Shiloh, a town in Ephraim, where "the temple of the Lord" was located at that time. The "temple" was actually "the tabernacle of the congregation" which Joshua had moved there from Gilgal (Joshua 4:19 and 18:1). Of course, the sacred "ark of the covenant" was in the tabernacle, or "temple."

THE MAN ELI:

History records Eli as a Levite, of the family of Ithamar, who was the youngest son of Aaron. Little is known of him apart from that which is found in 1 Samuel, chapters one through four.

Most (if not all) commentators designate him as the *high priest,* because of his descendancy, and the nature of his administration in the "temple." In the Scriptures, he is introduced to us in the story of Hannah and Elkanah, when they had come to Shiloh to worship and offer a sacrifice to God (1 Samuel 1:3, 9). The references to Eli are so woven into those about Samuel that we must endeavor (in this lesson) to concentrate our attention on Eli.

The first mention is with reference to his two sons, Hophni and Phinehas. *The Pulpit Commentary* suggests that "Eli apparently had devolved upon his sons his *priestly* functions, while he discharged the duties only of a *judge* . . . . " However, it seems safe to assume that he remained, *in fact,* the high priest as long as he lived.

At any rate, he was at the temple, and apparently in charge, when Elkanah made his offering and Hannah prayed her prayer for a son (1:9). Our first impression of Eli might be that he was a hard, unmerciful man; or at least, an undiscerning man.

A more charitable opinion might credit him with being a vigilant man. He was nearing seventy years of age, and possibly was less alert than in his younger days. Also, Israel's reputation for corrupt living was a well-known fact, however regrettable. It is not difficult to understand why he mistook Hannah's strange actions for drunkenness. We see the true spirit of the man in his words to her following her explanation:

"Then Eli answered and said, Go in peace: and the God of Israel grant thy petition that thou hast asked of him" (1:17). She did not tell him that she was praying for a son.

Nothing is recorded of Eli's attitude or response when the young Samuel was brought to the house of God, and was left there for training. Whatever "ministering" the child was capable of at so early an age is said to have been done " . . . unto the Lord before Eli the priest" (2:11). This would indicate that Eli accepted direct oversight of the child.

It would be paradoxical to say that Eli was *a fatherly poor father;* but it may have been true. Though his own sons had become "sons of Belial," he must have been known personally as a man with a good father's attributes. Hannah and Elkanah must have had confidence in him. (NOTE: The word "Belial" originally meant *worthless,* implying *recklessness* and *lawlessness.* Through much usage, it took on a certain "impersonation." The apostle Paul used the word once in this sense: "And what concord hath Christ with Belial?" (2 Corinthians 6:15). It was like equating the name with the Antichrist.)

Eli's sons are not under study in this lesson; but suffice it to say that they were dishonest in their handling of the sacrificial offerings of the people, acting in contempt of the law of God. They were robbers, both of the people and of God (1 Samuel 2:12-16). Also, they were adulterously immoral (2:22). Simply stated, "... *they knew not the Lord"* (2:12).

Through the centuries, men have passed critical judgment on Eli because of his wicked sons. He has been judged as weak; coddling; indulgent; too mild; too gentle; indifferent. It has been said that he only mildly *reproved* them when he should have *rebuked* them and taken the priesthood away from them.

It has been observed that no mention is made of his ever reproving them in the matter of the sacrifices; and that he spoke to them about their immoral, unchaste conduct only after "all the people" (2:23-25) brought him their complaints.

These judgmental conclusions seem fair and accurate, assuming that the Bible account gives the whole story. Josephus has practically nothing to say about the matter. But it is only being equitable to remember again Eli's age. He was "very old" at this point. We do not know how long these sons had been doing wickedly. Perhaps he had taught them well, and had put more confidence in them than was merited.

They may have been very *wily*—even *religious*—outwardly for awhile. There might have been a reluctance on the part of the people to go to the high priest and criticize his sons, who, after all, were also priests. Also, it is to be remembered that Israel, nationally, had been under the displeasure of God much of the time. In their long seasons of idol worship, lewd practices were a part of their "religion."

The fact is (if chronology is to be trusted) that the pronouncement made in Judges 13:1, in 1161 B.C., had not been lifted. To date, there had been no indication of a national repentance or an appeal to God for deliverance. The nation was still under the forty-five-year *Philistine Oppression.* Some individuals were doing their best to remain stedfast, but it cannot be assumed that sincere worship and holy living was the prevailing attitude.

None of this, however, excuses Eli's *light hand* on open sin. At the best, it shows why the *light hand* might have been taken so *lightly.* But for the sake of the righteous minority, God would intervene in due season. First, however, He would thoroughly refresh Eli's memory of things he really knew quite well.

A "man of God," a prophet, was sent by God with a message for the elderly priest and judge (1 Samuel 2:27-36). All arguments can now be put aside, for the prophet's message clearly reveals how Eli's conduct appeared in the sight of God.

The establishment of the priesthood in the wilderness was briefly but forcibly reviewed (2:27, 28). Aaron, the older brother of Moses, of the tribe of Levi, had been chosen as the first high priest. Through him the office was perpetuated, and the tribe of Levi was elevated above all the others. They were blessed with great wealth and high rank.

They were intrusted with a highly honorable and holy duty: " . . . to offer upon mine altar, to burn incense, to wear an ephod before me . . . " (2:28). These duties were actually privileges; and they were sacred indeed! The system of sacrifices and offerings represented the atonement for sins until the Messiah-Saviour should come. The "ephod," as was mentioned briefly concerning Gideon (Lesson Five), represented God's presence, and had a part in the revelation of His will through the wearer.

Their wealth derived from a generous share of the sacrificial offerings, and the tithes of all the people. Although it would have been a great privilege to fill the priestly offices even without remuneration, God had paid them well.

Then, leaving the "refresher course," the prophet, speaking for God ("Thus saith the Lord," verse 27), poses a pertinent question:

"Wherefore kick [profane, trample, spurn] ye at my sacrifice and at mine offering, which I have commanded in my habitation; and honourest thy sons above me, to make yourselves fat with the chiefest of all the offerings of Israel my people?" (2:29).

The Lord's question referred to very literal actions, as can be seen from verses 13 through 16. They showed no fearful respect in the way they carried out the offering process. They were concerned only in material profit, taking the best part ("chiefest") for themselves. In this way they made themselves "fat" financially, and probably physically. Someone has noted that Eli himself may have condoned his sons' wicked conduct by eating of their choice meat at their table—noting that it is included in Scripture that he was a "heavy" man (4:18).

The spiritual implications of the question were well known to Eli, as well as to every priest. The one and only answer need not be spoken. Only flagrant disobedience to God and apathetic neglect of sacred duty could account for Eli's attitude. It is clear that God saw him as an accomplice in the crimes of his sons; not that he approved of them, but he did not exercise his high priestly duty to keep the priesthood holy, even if a full purge were necessary! Perhaps this should make James' words weightier to us: "Therefore to him that knoweth to do good, and doeth it not, to him IT IS SIN"! (James 4:17).

The prophet then delivered *God's sentence*—"Wherefore the Lord God of Israel saith . . . . " The Lord recalled His promise of the perpetuality of the priesthood. (See Exodus 29:9 and Numbers 25:11-13.) *"But now . . . Be it far from me"* to honor the dishonorable! The *office* would remain forever, but *Eli's lineage* would not.

From that time forward, (1) their power ("arm") would diminish (verse 31), (2) their lives would be shortened (verses 31, 32), (3) an enemy—possibly the Philistines—would invade the habitation of God, or Israel (verse 32), and (4) those left of the house of Eli would become as beggars before their successor (verse 36).

Bible history shows that the decline was gradual, but sure. The far-reaching fulfillment was found to be in Christ, who was of the lineage of Judah, not Levi. But that was yet afar off. Commentators differ as to the meaning of the "faithful priest" of verse 35. While ultimately it was Christ, it is held that others were faithful in the interim; such as Samuel (who was a prophet, a priest, and a judge), and Zadok, in David's time.

Eli apparently accepted the prophet's words as inevitable. It seemed too late to alter the divine sentence. He was very old, and his eyes were growing dim. Only two more incidents are on record concerning him: (1) God's revelation about him to the child Samuel, and (2) his death.

Of the first, more will be said in the study of Samuel. Here it must be noted that Eli wisely instructed the lad when the Lord was trying to speak to him (3:9); and when the revelation turned out to be concerning Eli's judgment from the Lord, he was found to have submitted everything to God. "It is the Lord: let him do what seemeth him good" (3:18).

The second remaining incident began with an invasion by the Philistines in the region of Ebenezer and Aphek, probably in the general area of Samson's activities in Dan and northern Judah. The year was about 1141 B.C. Though it is not so stated, it would appear that Israel was once more trying to throw off the oppressors' yoke. However, no mention is made of repentance, or of their calling for God's help.

There were two major battles (1 Samuel 4:1, 2, 10). In the first battle, Israel lost about 4,000 men. The elders of Israel immediately began to search out the reason why the Lord had allowed this; but their searching was mostly through their own intellect. Almost as if by a "religiously" superstitious design, they decided that the physical presence of the ark of the covenant on the battlefield would invoke God's favor. So they sent for it to be brought from the tabernacle at Shiloh.

The ark was met with *great shouting* when it was brought into the camp, attended by the wicked sons of Eli—Hophni and Phinehas. The sound reverberated even to the Philistine camp. The Philistines feared the God of Israel (perhaps more than Israel feared Him)! Being idol worshippers, they equated "the *ark* of the Lord" with *God,* saying, *"God* is come into the camp . . . . Woe unto us!" (4:7, 8).

But, under the circumstances, they had nothing to fear, for God was working in another way! Israel was smitten again. The Israelites fled from the field—all but the 30,000 who fell! Worse yet, *"the ark of God was taken"!* Both Hophni and

Phinehas were slain, in fulfillment of the prophet's words (4:11).

At Shiloh, Eli was sitting by the wayside, watching and waiting for word from the battle. "... His heart trembled for the ark of God" (4:13). Apparently he had remained silent when the decision was made to carry it from its God-appointed place onto the field of battle. His *weakness* was showing again. Now it appears that he was actually expecting the worst.

A Benjamite runner brought the news of total defeat, and Eli heard the people of the city crying out in sorrow and alarm. "What meaneth the noise of this tumult?" he inquired. The messenger hurried to him with the tragic report:

"... Israel is fled before the Philistines, and there hath been a great slaughter among the people, and thy two sons also, Hophni and Phinehas, are dead, and the ark of God is taken."

The ninety-eight-year-old, dim-eyed high priest perhaps could have survived the news of the army's awful defeat, and even the death of his sons— which he probably expected. But when mention was made that the ark of God had fallen into Philistine hands, it was too much! "... He fell from off the seat backward...and his neck brake, and he died...."

And Phinehas' wife, dying from childbirth, "... named the child *Ichabod*.... and she said, *The glory is departed from Israel:* for the ark of God is taken" (4:21, 22).

FOR OUR ADMONITION AND LEARNING:

The mishandling of Church matters, whether finances or sacramental functions, tend to drive people from the house of God. Satan uses such things to his advantage, making men and women to *abhor* that which God has designed to be *enjoyed*. Allowing sin—or even folly—among the leadership can tear down much faster than we can build!

"Open rebuke is better than secret love" (Proverbs 27:5), and "Them that sin rebuke before all, that others also may fear" (1 Timothy 5:20), is not meant only for *other people's children*. (Read Deuteronomy 13:6-11.) While it is true that we deal with sin differently under grace, it still must be dealt with *impartially*. Because of Calvary, God has every right to be a jealous God. "He that loveth father and mother... son or daughter more than me is not worthy of me" (Matthew 10:37). Surely Eli knew these things.

We are often prone to mistake the *officer* for the *office*. Sinning ministers do not make *the office of the minister* sinful. Again, Satan takes advantage, and turns innocent and unthinking people away from *true religion*.

No sacred symbol, or relic, can protect a sinful bearer, or wearer, from the just and equitable judgment of God. If the heart is right, even "the ark of the covenant" cannot add anything to the favor the justified person has with God.

The sons of Eli "knew not the Lord," yet they were in the priestly office. The outcome is sure to be less than commendable when a man who knows not the Lord by the new birth is put in a ministerial office. Yet it is not uncommon. In such a capacity, one thing can be worse than *knowing not the Lord*. That is, to *know* Him (or to have known Him), yet *live more corruptly* than those who have never known Him!

Shouting for joy in the Spirit is one thing; *shouting in the flesh* is something else! The people shouted over the "ark," not so much because of its true significance, but in the hope that something about its presence would bribe God to favor Israel. But *Israel was displeasing to God;* so neither the ark nor the shouting were of any help!

—Lesson Eleven—

SAMUEL: THE FIFTEENTH JUDGE

Part I

Suggested Scripture Readings: 1 Samuel 1-8.

Helps in Pronunciation: Ramathaim-zophim—RA-math-A-im-ZO-fim; Ephrathites—EF-ra-thites; Peninnah—pe-NIN-ah; Abinadab—a-BIN-a-dab; Kirjath-jearim—KER-jath-JEE-a-rim; Eleazer—EL-ee-A-zer; Abiah—a-BI-ah.

THE HISTORICAL SITUATION:

We have noted considerable chronological overlapping in the last several judgeships. If we go back to Samuel's birthdate in about 1170 B.C., he lived contemporarily with Jair, Jephthah, Ibzan, Elon, Abdon, Samson, and Eli. This means that Israel was fluctuating from apostasy to serving the Lord, then back to apostasy. It seems apparent that different tribal areas were affected in different ways, and that some families remained true to God even though their tribe or nation had gone after idols.

From the reading of 1 Samuel alone, one finds practically nothing about the judgeships of those in the *Book of the Judges*. Though Samson (the last judge in the *Book of the Judges*) died in about 1120 B.C., no mention is made there of Samuel, who must have been fifty years old at the time.

It is evident that the tribes intermingled a great deal. After all, they were all Israelites. But we, in our time of "instant communication," can hardly comprehend the degree of isolation that existed in those earlier centuries.

The locale of Samuel's family was in Ramathaim-zophim (Ramah) of Ephraim. This was about twenty-five miles west of Shiloh. The tabernacle of the congregation was at Shiloh, and Samuel's family went there yearly to sacrifice unto the Lord (1 Samuel 1:3). From 1 Chronicles 6:16, 23, we learn that they were of the tribe of Levi. Being "Ephrathites" meant only that this Levite family lived in the inherited area of the tribe of Ephraim. The Levites had no restricted land inheritance.

From our study of Eli, we learned that the Philistines were plaguing this area of Israel, and that this oppression continued for forty years. Samuel was a young man at the time of Eli's death following a devastating battle with the Philistines. This indicates the kind of times in which Samuel grew up. Strangely enough, Israel was wanting God's help, but nothing is said about their having repented of their idolatry since the time prior to Samson's rule.

In the first of two lessons on Samuel, we will cover the first eight chapters of 1 Samuel, the time period being about 1171 to 1095 B.C., or seventy-six years. We will find that Samuel was a *prophet* and *priest,* as well as Israel's last *judge.* We can only roughly estimate when each of these ministries began. It is not necessary to belabor the point too much.

THE MAN SAMUEL:

Samuel's birth was on this wise: A Levite man by the name of Elkanah, and his two wives, Peninnah and Hannah, went from their home in Ramathaim-zophim to Shiloh to make their yearly offering to God in the temple, or tabernacle. Hannah was barren, but Peninnah had children. Peninnah seemed to derive a hateful pleasure from provoking Hannah with taunts about her childlessness. Because of this, the annual feast was much less than joyful for Hannah. She wept, and did not eat.

Elkanah loved Hannah, apparently more than he did Peninnah. He did his best to console her, suggesting that his love for her was so great that it should equal ten sons. But the bitterness of Hannah's soul was so intense that she wept and prayed before the Lord, and made a self-denying vow:

"O Lord of hosts, if thou wilt indeed look on the affliction of thine handmaid, and remember me, and not forget thine handmaid, but wilt give unto thine handmaid a man child, then I will give him unto the Lord all the days of his life, and there shall no razor come upon his head" (1 Samuel 1:11).

Eli, the high priest, "sat upon a seat by the post of the temple" (1:9). His attention was attracted to Hannah as she continued praying. He was suspicious—even displeased. He concluded that she was drunk. Why? Was it her unusually long prayer? Was it not the custom to pray silently? Did the expression on her face seem contorted by the anguish of her soul? Possibly the Spirit moved her in such a way as to make her seem unbalanced in body, as by the effects of strong drink. Eli may have reasoned that she was one of the vile women who visited Hophni and Phinehas—"sons of Belial" —even at the door of the tabernacle (1 Samuel 2:12, 22). When Eli had censured Hannah, he was satisfied with her explanation, though she did not tell him that her prayer was for a son. He pronounced a blessing upon her, and she went her way and took some nourishment. She must have felt some assurance that her prayer and Eli's blessing had been heard in heaven. Next morning after worship, they returned to Ramah.

In due process of time the son was born and was named Samuel, meaning "asked of God." Hannah kept her vow, first only in her heart, for it was only reasonable that the child should not be taken to Shiloh and left at the temple until he was weaned and old enough to be placed in the hands of others. But when he was possibly three years old (some think he may have been eight or nine), he was left at the temple with Eli. It was only then that the high priest learned of Hannah's request (1:24-28).

It is heart-warming to note Elkanah's concurrence in Hannah's promise to God (1:21-28). Each year the mother made their Nazarite son "a little coat," and took it to him at the time of the yearly sacrifice. Undoubtedly the two of them visited their young son together and made the loving presentation. It must have been an awesome experience seeing one so young ministering before the Lord, and girded with a linen ephod—a Levite garment. Still, Samuel probably looked forward to these annual visits with increasing understanding of it all.

The smile of God shone through on this devoted couple as time went on:

"And the Lord visited Hannah, so that she conceived, and bare three sons and two daughters. And the child Samuel grew before the Lord" (2:21).

We must not overlook the providential finger of God in all the circumstances surrounding the birth of Samuel. His adult life as an instrument of God testifies to the movement of the Divine Hand, from Hannah's barrenness, through the making of the solemn vow, and on to his very early ministry before the high priest in the one and only "tabernacle of the congregation." Israel needed revival. The priesthood was defiled. The people were like sheep without an able shepherd. The tribes were becoming more and more independent of one another; in fact, at times they warred against one another. The judges had been "channels of blessing"—from time to time, and here and there. But God needed a man "of His own design," as it were. The beautiful story of Hannah, Elkanah, and Samuel is the unveiling of that design. It is wonderful indeed!

The atmosphere into which the tender Samuel was thrust was that of a distressing mixture of good and evil. We have studied Eli, as a priest and judge, and as an overly indulgent father. Perhaps he was wise enough to keep some distance between his young charge and his own dishonest, immoral sons. Then, the purer minds of Israel were certainly faithful in the tabernacle worship, as better examples. Still it is unrealistic to think that a growing, maturing youth would not be exposed to, and aware of, the conduct of Hophni and Phinehas. Their inconsistencies could hardly have gone unnoticed by one who was undergoing special training for God's ministry. Surely he was taught the Law, both its moral and its ceremonial aspects.

The contrast is glaring: "Now the sons of Eli were sons of Belial; they knew not the Lord.... Wherefore the sin of the young men was very great before the Lord.... But Samuel ministered before the Lord.... And the child Samuel grew on, and was in favour both with the Lord, and also with men" (2:12, 17, 18, 26).

The Nazarite vow, the daily prayers of his parents, and the pre-ordained will of God all worked together to keep the heart and mind pure. In the meantime, God was dealing with Eli about his slack hand with his sons, sending a prophet to reprove him, and to declare that his house would be cut off from its lineage in the priesthood (2:27-36).

At this point we come to a great leap forward in Samuel's destiny. His age, as suggested by chronologists, is a matter of uncertainty. However, it would seem important. If he was born in 1170 B.C., the *Thomspon Chain-Reference Bible* date at the beginning of chapter three (1165 B.C.) seems unimaginative. While there is no doubt that God could have made His message understood by a five-year-old child, it seems to lack precedent. Considering that the chronologist leaves a twenty-four-year lapse between chapters three and four (1165 to 1141 B.C.), we are made to wonder if the date might apply to verse one, but not necessarily to the specific event related in the rest of the chapter.

Josephus says, "Now when Samuel was *twelve years old,* he began to *prophesy:* and once when he was asleep, God called him by his name...." One commentator adds: "In later times this age was a critical point in the life of a Jewish boy. He then became 'a son of the Law,' and was regarded as personally responsible for obedience to it. It was at the age of twelve that 'the child Jesus' first went up to Jerusalem along with His parents."

The story of Samuel's call (1 Samuel 3:2-18) is well know by every Sunday school boy or girl. It is probably more significant than usually supposed that God so directly involved Eli in his dealing with Samuel. At the very least, it relieved the child of any legitimate suspicion. God did not speak (except to call Samuel's name) until Eli had concluded that He was calling the youth, and had instructed him as to how he should respond. One unidentified commentator has said:

"The call of Samuel was the first step toward superseding Eli, and putting another and more faithful person in his room. It was necessary therefore that Eli should be assured ... that it was the beginning of the fulfillment of God's threatenings against himself [1 Samuel 2:27-36]. And how could this be done more forcibly or more naturally than by allowing Samuel to mistake God's voice for Eli's ... ?"

A twelve-year-old youth of Samuel's caliber spiritually could comprehend God's message, even though it was decidedly on the adult level. It is probable that verse seven (of chapter three) is significant in relationship to the change reflected in Samuel's call. Certainly we are not to understand that "Samuel did not yet know the Lord" meant the same thing as was said of Hophni and Phinehas (2:12). Relating the statement to verse one—"And the word of the Lord was precious in those days; there was no open vision"—we may understand that Samuel was about to come to know the Lord as a God of direct revelation, which had been rare and unusual throughout the *Period of the Judges.*

God's word to Samuel (3:11-14) may or may not have surprised him. It seems clear that he fully comprehended it, though perhaps not all of its implications. However, there was a awesome element which would have astounded men of any age and of any time! At the third call, there was more than a voice: "And *the Lord came,* and *stood,* and *called"* (verse 10). Verse 15 speaks of *"the vision,"* indicating a visible presence of the Lord.

As to the understanding, it must have become clear as "Samuel lay until the morning," pondering it all in the light of the things his alert eyes and mind had observed for several years; reprehensible things which had continued without rebuke and without dismissal of the guilty! When Eli pressed Samuel for the message, and had heard "every whit" of it, he acknowledged the truth of it, and submitted himself to God's ultimatum.

Undoubtedly we are to understand this experience as Samuel's call as a *prophet,* as Eli must have perceived it also. "Samuel grew" (3:19), in stature and understanding, for "the Lord was with him, and did let none of his words fall to the ground." It is not that the Lord obligated Himself to bring to pass every word Samuel prophesied. Rather, Samuel spoke only as God dictated, and God confirmed His Word, thereby establishing Samuel in the minds of "all Israel" as a true "prophet of the Lord" (3:20).

A new intercourse with God was opened up. Chapter three begins by saying, *"the Word of the Lord* was precious [scarce, rare] in those days." It ends with, "the Lord revealed himself to Samuel in Shiloh by *the Word of the Lord."* There had been occasional prophets in past generations. From this time forward, prophets would fill a continuous role in God's dispensation of His Word. It has been well said, "Samuel was the last of the Judges and the first of the Prophets."

Samuel's "training ministry" was now complete and his "official ministry" as a prophet had begun. "And the word of Samuel came to *all Israel."* But Israel would be slow to recognize this, as the entire fourth chapter clearly shows.

Eli's "handwriting on the wall" probably was known to none but himself and Samuel. He was still the high priest and judge. Hophni and Phinehas had not been unseated. Israel had looked to Eli for eighty years. They may have done very much as they pleased, since the aged high priest was known for his leniency, and, in later years, for his apathy and negligence. Samuel was not yet officially their "judge." This would have caused a confusing dividing of their loyalties.

Chapters four, five and six deal with a very distressing period in Israel's history, but Samuel's name is not mentioned. We studied the Philistine invasion in Lesson Ten, ending with Israel's defeat, the loss of 34,000 men, the taking of the ark of the covenant, and the deaths of Eli and his two sons. The ark remained in Philstine hands for seven months (6:1). So much trouble befell them that they, with considerable difficulty, ridded themselves of it. Eventually, it came to rest in the house of Abinadab at Kirjath-jearim, perhaps twenty-five miles southwest of Shiloh. They sanctified a priest, Eleazer (Abinadab's son) "to keep the ark of the Lord" (7:1). It remained there twenty years.

Between the first two verses of chapter seven, these twenty years expired. However strange it may seem that Samuel's activities go unmentioned, the chronology bears it out that way. Much conjecturing would not be edifing. We know only that Israel was in lamentation during that time. The Philistines' over-whelming victory (chapter four) had subdued them. The loss of the ark had discouraged them to the extent that even after it was in Israelite hands, but not in the tabernacle, they remained so spiritually low that they made no effort to restore the national worship. They were reaping the awful harvest of their spiritual instability—yes, from the passing of Joshua until now!

We have seen that Samuel, from his childhood, was one to carry on his "ministry" submissively; he did not push himself forward. If he was needed, he would be there. But although Israel *knew* that God had established him as a prophet (3:30), and though his word came to all Israel (4:1), we do not read that Israel *sought* his help or advice for twenty years! We can only assume that Samuel patiently waited upon the Lord, serving as judge of those who came to him; and that the Lord waited for Israel to humble themselves before Him.

It was about 1120 B.C. when Samuel spoke at last (7:3). God's time had come, and He had his man ready. Israel was ripe for repentance. It seems incredible that many of them were still worshipping Baalim and Ashtaroth, even while they "lamented after the Lord" and recognized His presence in the ark of the covenant. But now they were so full of the fruits of their fleshly lusts that it was *coming out of their nostrils,* as it were (Numbers 11:18-20, 31-33).

Samuel's message was just simple, basic "evangelism" —quit serving other gods, prepare your hearts, and serve the Lord only. This they did, along with prayer and fasting, and the confession, *"We have sinned against the Lord"* (7:6).

And there at Mizpeh it is written that "Samuel *judged* the children of Israel." Verse fifteen states that "Samuel judged Israel all the days of his life," evidently meaning from that time until his death.

Now that Israel had hearkened to Him through Samuel, their sincerity was put to a test. The Philistines were never slack in watching Israel's every move, so their eye was on the gathering at Mizpeh about fifteen miles south of Shiloh. It is not said that Israel had gathered with war in mind; but God was directing.

The Philistines ran no risk. They sent out an army, probably hoping to frighten Israel into continued submission. But frightened and repentant Israel cried out to Samuel for prayer (7:8). Samuel took his time. He killed a lamb and offered it as a burnt-offering. (Here he filled *the priestly office.* He was now *prophet, priest,* and *judge.)* While the ceremony was still in progress, the Philistines drew near for battle.

Now that the Lord knew Israel was trusting in Him, He intervened in their behalf. He "thundered with a great thunder . . . and discomfited [frustrated, confused] them; and they were smitten before Israel" (7:10). Josephus says there was also an earthquake. His description of the discomfiture is graphic indeed!

You will remember that God "discomfited" Sisera and his host in the battle with Deborah and Barak (Judges 4:15). Here again, the Lord fought for Israel. And, as on that former occasion, Israel pursued the enemy so that they were subdued so thoroughly that "they came no more into the coast of Israel." (We will study this further in Lesson Twelve.)

After this victory, Samuel set up a stone near Mizpeh and called it Ebenezer, meaning "Hitherto hath the Lord helped us." Then he established a circuit of cities in which to judge the people. These were: Bethel, Gilgal, and Mizpeh (7:16)—all historical locations. Verse seventeen indicates that Ramah, his home city, was also a part of the circuit, for "there he judged Israel; and there he built an altar unto the Lord." Josephus says he traveled the circuit twice a year.

It seems that about eight years had passed between the victory at Mizpeh and the beginning of chapter eight. If so, it was about 1112 B.C., and Samuel is spoken of as being "old"—about fifty-eight years old. Evidently to relieve himself of heavy responsibilities, he made his sons, Joel and Abiah, judges and stationed them in Beer-sheba, perhaps fifty miles southwest of Ramah. Thus did the solution of one problem create a greater one!

However upright these sons may have been prior to this time, *covetousness* soon possessed them once they were intrusted with judgeships. Their love of money tempted them to get it the easy way—by taking bribes, or "pay-offs." When this was done, righteous judgment of the people was naturally perverted. Whoever had the most money was favored by the judge! Even if this were their only fault, it made them corrupt in the eyes of God and the people. And the people rightfully complained. However, in "filing their complaint," they "attached a rider," so to speak, which was grievous to Samuel:

"Behold, thou art old, and thy sons walk not in thy ways: now make us a king to judge us like all the nations" (8:5).

Apparently the request for a king was so devastating to Samuel's spirit that the problem about his sons seemed unimportant by comparison. He went to God in prayer. Of course, God had known the thoughts of their hearts long before they were voiced. His answer must have surprised Samuel. It indicated that Samuel may have taken the people's request as a personal affront to his judgeship; but God knew that Israel's complaint was as old as Adam: *Depraved men are rebels against God!*

But after all, Samuel had not yet experienced one full lifetime of dealing with this erring nation. God had already "suffered long" with them—from the day He had made them His people! As though this were *just another rebellion,* He said to Samuel:

"... Hearken unto the voice of the people in all that they say unto thee: for they have not rejected *thee,* but they have rejected *me,* that I should not reign over them.

"According to all the works which they have done since the day that I brought them up out of Egypt even unto this day, wherewith they have forsaken me, and served other gods, so do they also unto thee.

"Now therefore hearken unto their voice: howbeit yet protest solemnly unto them, and shew them the manner of the king that shall reign over them" (8:7-9).

God had come to Samuel's aid in telling him how to handle the situation. If Samuel had himself opposed the people's suggestion, they could have accused him of lusting after power and authority; and of wanting to further indulge his sons, who would have no office under the desired king. If he had himself yielded to their request, he should have felt that he was bending under fleshly pressure and failing God's expectations of him.

But now, he relayed *God's words* to Israel, carefully showing them the consequences of living under a monarch (8:10-18). He concluded by warning them that God would not hear them when eventually they would cry out to Him in complaint against their king (8:18). But they were determined.

"... Nay; but WE WILL HAVE a king over us;

"That we also may be *like all the nations;* and that our *king* may *judge* us, and go out before us, and *fight our battles*" (8:20).

After another prayer, and reassurance from God, "Samuel said unto the men of Israel, Go ye every man unto his city."

The matter was in God's hands. All must await His next direction.

FOR OUR ADMONITION AND LEARNING:

It is not good to mete out premature judgment on people's actions, unless they are obviously evil. Eli was totally wrong about Hannah's movements in the tabernacle.

We lose nothing by giving or "lending" to the Lord. Hannah and Elkanah were given sevenfold for the total dedication of one son to God.

The "externals" of worship give little satisfaction. With the "ark" missing from the tabernacle, the ceremonial rites of the atonement lacked much of their true meaning. The "ark" represented God's presence. In Christian worship, the prayers and preaching may be *eloquent,* the music and singing very *professional,* and the lip-service of praise and testimony nicely *"learned,"* but without *the true presence of God by His Spirit,* we return home "empty."

Israel continued harboring their idols, even while *lamenting after the Lord* and *grieving over the ark.* Theirs was only "a form of godliness" without the power of God. They were really saying, "Bless me, but let me do as I please." "They feared the Lord [for selfish ends], and served their own gods, after the manner of the nations" (2 Kings 17:33).

Office-seekers are often changed from "acceptable candidates" to "corrupt politicians" by temptations to "the good life"—the rich, indulgent life! And the "office" may be in the Church as well as in the government! Good leaders who will *remain good* are always in demand.

—Lesson Twelve—

SAMUEL: THE FIFTEENTH JUDGE

Part II

Suggested Scripture Readings: 1 Samuel 9:13; 15, 16; 19:18-24; 25:1; 28.

Helps in Pronunciation: Gibeah—GIB-e-ah; Eliab—e-LI-ab; Naioth—NA-oth; Endor—EN-dor.

THE HISTORICAL SITUATION:

Apparently the forty years of the *Second Philistine Oppression* (1161 to 1141 B.C.) ended with the victory at Mizpeh, or Ebenezer (1 Samuel 7:10-14). This does not mean that the Philistines were totally vanquished; but they were "subdued" (7:13) and stopped their invasions for a time. We will see that they continued as *thorns in the sides* of Israel, though not victorious any more in Samuel's lifetime.

Now a new era begins in Israel's history. They have rejected the theocracy, and God has granted their demand for a king. The new era dates from about 1095 B.C., which apparently was the year when the king was anointed. The chronology at the time of this transition seems to include some assumption. The events of Chapter 8 seem to have begun about 1112 B.C., but the anointing of Saul is calculated to have been in 1095 B.C. This seventeen-year interim assumes that a number of years passed with Samuel's sons as judges, giving time for them to make their "perverted judgment" generally known and felt. Events may have moved along more slowly than it would seem from a casual reading, chapter by chapter. In fact, some time may have elapsed between chapters eight and nine. God may not have been *in a hurry* about revealing to the people who their king would be.

It appears that the overall plan of God included a "king" for Israel in due time. Early prophecies showed the power would shift to the tribe of Judah, out of which *Christ the King* would come. And when He came, He spoke constantly in terms of a "kingdom."

But Israel's demand was premature. In fact, it was a usurpation of the authority of God. If and when a "kingdom" were in order, God should have been the Initiator. And had He been, it is almost certain that that kingdom would not have been one "like all the nations." It would have been (and eventually will be) a *kingdom* as unique as was the original *theocracy.* However, since Israel had rejected the Divine order, they would have to live with the consequences. Once the "kingdom" took on the characteristics of the contemporary powers round about them, the pattern persisted, even through the reigns of God-called men like David, Solomon, and a few others.

1095 B.C. (as chronologists fix it) was to be an eventful year, including the selection of the king, his anointing (chapter ten), his eventual "coming out" and establishing himself in the minds of the people (chapter 11), and the formal proclamation of the kingdom (chapter 12). Samuel officiated in every instance. He continued as *prophet* and *priest,* and evidently in some measure as *judge,* since it was said of him that he "judged Israel all the days of his life" (7:15). God had appointed him; and God recognized His appointments to the end.

THE MAN SAMUEL:

On a certain day, Samuel started to "the high place" (where the altar of the Lord was located at Ramah), and he met a man and his servant, who was looking for him. The Lord had told Samuel the day before:

"To-morrow about this time I will send thee a man out of the land of Benjamin, and thou shalt anoint him to be captain over my people Israel, that he may save my people out of the hand of the Philistines: for I have looked upon my people, because their cry is come unto me" (1 Samuel 9:16). (NOTE: The "subdued" Philistines would still plague Israel from time to time. The people would never feel at rest concerning them until they should be totally driven out. Saul would be in power for forty years, so we are not to expect an immediate victory.)

The man seeking Samuel was Saul (9:1, 2). As soon as Samuel saw him, the Lord said to him, "Behold the man whom I spake to thee of! this same shall reign over my people."

Now Saul was trying to find his father's lost asses; but in all probability it was God who had caused them to go astray in order that Saul would go in search of them, eventually coming to Samuel's city. And it was probably God who made the servant suggest that the "seer" (Samuel, the prophet) might be able to direct them in their search (9:6).

At any rate, they stood before the aged prophet, whose words must have been quite surprising:

". . . Ye shall eat with me to-day, and to-morrow I will let thee go, and will tell thee all that is in thine heart.

"As for thine asses that were lost three days ago . . . they are found. An on whom is all the desire of Israel? Is it not on thee, and on all thy father's house?"

Most commentators insist that Saul thought Samuel spoke in jest, possibly because of Saul's height. Josephus describes him thus: " . . . A young man of comely countenance, and of a tall body, but his understanding and his mind were preferable to what was visible in him . . . . " On a later occasion it is said that "he was higher than any of the people from his shoulders upward" (10:23). It is likely that Saul vaguely understood what the prophet intended, but his modesty refused to let him take it seriously.

As the evening progressed, all seemed strange. Samuel invited Saul and his servant to a feast, and thirty guests were there—probably distinguished persons, since it seems clear that Samuel had planned it all because of the Lord's words to him the day before. Though the guests were there, and Saul was only a "drop-in" who had chanced to come that way, yet everything had been planned around him (9:22-24).

After the feast at the high place, Samuel talked with Saul, probably alone, on the housetop. That he spent the night at Samuel's home is clear from verses 25 and 26. Samuel was directing every move, and all others were at his command. Sending Saul away, he accompanied him to the edge of town. The servant was told to go on ahead, and Samuel said privately to Saul, " . . . Stand thou still a while, that I may shew thee the word of God." If Saul had indeed thought until now that the prophet had merely been unnecessarily courteous, or had been enjoying a little humor at his expense, so to speak, the time had come to put all such out of mind. Samuel anointed him with oil, kissed him, and said, "Is it not because the Lord hath anointed thee to be captain over his inheritance?" (10:1).

All of the seer's words of the evening before, and all of his own remonstration as to his small tribe and insignificant family probably flashed through Saul's mind. He could not entertain the thought that the prophet would extend his jest to involve the priestly anointing privilege. But to erase any lingering doubt, Samuel gave him three signs of immediately upcoming events (10:2-7), that he might know that God had spoken to the prophet. Then he gave a direction which, in the after outworking of events, appears to have been a prophecy to be fulfilled at Gilgal (13:8-10). The "seven days" of this direction (10:8) does not seem to have any reference to another gathering at Gilgal to "renew the kingdom" (11:14, 15ff).

"And it was so, that when he had turned his back to go from Samuel, God gave him another heart: and all those signs came to pass that day" (10:9).

The third sign involved the Spirit of the Lord coming upon him, and his prophesying with "a company of prophets" (10:5, 6). The "hill of God" mentioned in verse five is said to have been a common reference to the city of Gibeah, where Saul lived. Thus many of his acquaintances were present, and were surprised that he prophesied. They interpreted it to mean that God had called him to be a prophet. Evidently Saul now knew that Samuel had known for sure that he was anointed the ruler of Israel. But he kept his secret. Even when his uncle endeavored to learn the meaning of his meeting with Samuel, he mentioned only that Samuel had told them the asses had been found.

Now, Samuel called the people together at Mizpeh (one of the circuit cities). It was one thing for him to obey the Lord's instructions to him about the king; but it would be quite another thing to convince the people. This would be his first effort to that end. He began by relaying God's words to them; reproving, yet condescending words:

"Thus saith the Lord God of Israel, I brought up Israel out of Egypt, and delivered you out of the hand of the Egyptians, and out of the hands of all kingdoms, and of them that oppressed you:

"And ye have this day rejected your God, who himself saved you out of all your adversities and your tribulations; and ye have said unto him, Nay, but set a king over us . . . " (1 Samuel 10:18, 19).

To relieve Samuel of any seeming personal preferment in the appointment, God ordered that the selection be made publicly by lot. In the end, the lot fell on Saul (10:21), but he didn't come forth. The Lord used this as an added confirmation of His hand in the selection. When the people sought Him concerning Saul's absence, He said, "Behold, he hath hid himself among the stuff." And true to this word from God, he was found and brought forth. See him, in your imagination, standing embarrassingly modest, head and shoulders above the crowd! Samuel said:

"See ye him whom the Lord hath chosen, that there is none like him among all the people?"

Generally speaking, the people were greatly pleased, and they all shouted, *"God save the king!"*

Then Samuel reminded them again of "the manner of the kingdom," and it was written (perhaps as "minutes of the meeting") and laid up before the Great Witness on high. And the crowd dispersed, some going with Saul to Gibeah, "with him" both in person and in heart. But, as usual, there was also "the opposition"—doubters concerning this "home-town-boy-made-good"—despisers, perhaps through jealousy. But Saul "held his peace" (10:27).

We will pass over the war with the Ammonites (chapter 11), since we are studying Samuel, not Saul. However, we should note that Saul, little in his own sight, but with the Spirit of God upon him, mentioned Samuel's authority along with his own, in calling his army together. Some think that Samuel went with him to war, but this is conjecture. But when the war was won, the people were so thrilled with their king that they appealed to Samuel to bring forth those opposers (10:27). and put them to death; but Saul would not allow this to be done.

Samuel was doing all in his power to support Saul, and to honor him before the people. Following this victory over the Ammonites, he called for another gathering at Gilgal to "renew the kingdom" (11:14, 15). Gilgal was another one of the "circuit cities," somewhat removed from the others. Possibly large numbers of the people could be there who were not at the Mizpeh gathering, and the king would become more widely known and accepted. Apparently the venture was a great success.

It was possibly on the same day that Samuel spoke very plainly to "all Israel" (12:1), declaring once more that, although they had asked for a king, and were now rejoicing in him, God was not pleased with what they had done.

First, he evoked a witness from them of his own integrity and uprightness through the many years he had been their prophet, priest, and judge (12:2, 3). They all concurred that there was nothing but good to be said of him.

Next, rehearsing their history briefly (12:6-13), he caused them to understand that, though God had been their Great King, they had rejected Him in favor of an earthly king. But despite all of this, if they and their king would fear the Lord, serve Him, obey His voice, and not rebel against His commandments, He would let them continue as His followers (12:14). If not, His hand would be against them (verse 15).

Then, that they might perceive that their wickedness was great in asking for a king (12:17), Samuel called upon God to give them a sign. It was the time of the wheat harvest, when it was a thing virtually unknown to have thunder and rain. But he called on the Lord to send thunder and rain, and the Lord sent it!

The people confessed their sin in the fear of God, and begged that Samuel pray that they would not die; for they knew full well that *death* was the Law's penalty for *sin!* Samuel told them that they need not far death if they would not turn aside from following the Lord, but would serve Him with all their heart (12:20). He promised to pray for them, for not to do so would have been a sin on his part. He closed by saying:

"But if ye shall still do wickedly, ye shall be consumed, both ye and your king."

The Bible doesn't keep us wondering how the king turned out. First Samuel, chapter thirteen, relates an incident which happened "when he had reigned two years over Israel." At the time of his anointing, the Lord had told Samuel that Saul should save Israel out of the hand of the Philistines (9:16). We are not told that Samuel mentioned this to Saul. But now the king raised up something of a "standing army," as any nation would do. However, it appears that the successful bout with the Ammonites may have gone to Saul's head.

Chapter thirteen, verses two through seven, seem to relate a regrettable bungling in military affairs; but we are here concerned with Samuel's role.

As stated earlier, a meeting of Samuel with Saul at Gilgal was on God's agenda, at some indefinite time (10:8). Had Samuel spoken these directives in the spirit of prophecy? The gathering in chapter 11, verses 14 and 15, could hardly have been intended, for on that occasion there had been no reason for *a seven-day waiting period;* neither did Samuel tell Saul *what he should do.*

Now, after two years, we find a meeting at Gilgal (13:8-10), which Saul apparently thought was the one predicted; especially when he had waited a week for Samuel's appearance. Restless and distrustful, he became agitated because Samuel had not come when he had expected him—though Samuel actually was not late. He took upon himself the duties of the priestly office and offered the sacrifice; but Samuel came immediately after the ceremony had ended!

There were volumes of meaning in Samuel's first words, evidently spoken in astonishment: "WHAT HAST THOU DONE?" In reply, Saul poured forth his "logic," insinuating that Samuel had not kept his word, and maintaining that he literally had to *force* himself to do what seemed necessary to do.

What was Samuel's reply to all of this "pious rationalism"? "THOU HAST DONE FOOLISHLY . . . . " Saul had not obeyed God's law pertaining to the priesthood! Furthermore, he had not obeyed God's directive through His prophet!

The penalty? His family lineage in the kingly succession was discontinued. He had replaced honor with infamy. God would give the throne to a man "after His own heart." The grounds of the verdict were pure and simple: " . . . Because thou has not kept that which the Lord commanded thee" (13:14).

With that, Samuel left Saul to "live with it"!

But for Israel's sake, and for His great name's sake, God granted some victories over the Philistines, and others. Saul's son Jonathan was a righteous man; and God would honor his efforts in behalf of his father. But Saul blundered on in his "religious flesh"; still, God was merciful to His people. So time passed, with "sore war against the Philistines all the days of Saul" (14:52)—and the remaining words of the verse are revealing: Saul's eye was only on the "strong" and "valiant." There seemed little concern about faith and trust in the wisdom and might of the Almighty God!

If Saul learned anything from Samuel's reproof at Gilgal, the memory of it diminished with the years. God's merciful deliverances probably seemed more and more his own! So, some fourteen years later (about 1079 B.C.) we find him again in trouble with God.

The Lord sent Samuel to him with specific orders. It was the time of God's vengeance on the Amalekites for their past treatment of Israel. The orders were:

"Thus saith the Lord of hosts.... Now go and smite Amalek, and *utterly destroy* all that they *have,* and spare *them* not; but slay both man and woman, infant and suckling, ox and sheep, camel and ass" (15:2, 3).

With an army of 210,000, Saul went forth and did as God had said through Samuel—EXCEPT—! "But Saul and the people spared Agag [the king of the Amalekites], and the best of the sheep, and of the oxen, and of the fatlings, and lambs, and all that was good, and would not *utterly destroy* them...."

Of course, the Lord saw it and was grieved; and He spoke to Samuel: "It repenteth me that I have set up Saul to be king: for he is turned back from following me, and hath not performed my commandments." Samuel was grieved also, and he prayed all night. In the morning he learned that Saul had moved from the Amalekite territory in southeastern Judah to Gilgal, a journey of perhaps fifty miles. So Samuel went to Gilgal to confront him.

Saul came out "praising" the Lord even as he spoke a lie—at best, it was less than a half-truth! "Blessed be thou of the Lord: I have performed the commandment of the Lord" (15:13).

"And Samuel said, What meaneth then this bleating of the sheep in mine ears, and the lowing of the oxen which I hear?"

Saul had not forgotten how to employ his "philosophical piety." He had also learned to charge others with his sins. *"They ... the people ... "* (verse 15). But Samuel had another word for Saul from God! Boldly he said, *"Stay!"* In other words, "I will hear no more of your pretentious prattle!" Then he delivered God's message (15:17-19, 22, 23).

It was weighty with the things that mattered most to God: "... When thou wast little in thine own sight...." "Wherefore then didst thou not obey... but didst fly upon the spoil...?" "To obey is better than sacrifice, and to hearken than the fat of rams." "Rebellion...stubbornness...." Then, once again the ultimatum:

"Because thou hast rejected the word of the Lord, he hath also rejected thee from being king."

Saul then admitted his sin, but laid the cause on the people. He asked Samuel for pardon, wanting him to worship with him. But Samuel turned to leave. Saul, in a sort of egotistical desperation, laid hold on him and rent his mantle. Samuel used the incident to remind Saul that the Lord had rent the kingdom from him that day, and already had given it to his successor!

Then Saul changed his ploy: "I have sinned: yet honour me... before... my people..." (verse 30). What a miserable thought! He must finish his reign, responsible to the people, yet would in fact not be king in the eyes of God! A "front" was all he could offer from that time on!

After Samuel had slain Agag, he went home to Ramah, and "came no more to see Saul until the day of his death." However, he mourned for him, no doubt remembering the days when the big, tall king was little, or humble, in his own sight.

Apparently Samuel's "mourning" for Saul had more than satisfied the Lord, for He asked him how long he intended to continue it. The future must be provided for. So God sent Samuel to the home of Jesse, at Bethlehem, to anoint a new king from among his sons (16:1). Samuel was afraid Saul would hear of it and kill him; but the Lord told him to take a sacrifice. Nothing would be thought of a priest offering a sacrifice.

When he arrived at Bethlehem, the elders feared lest he had come to prophesy of coming trouble; but Samuel assured them that he had come peaceably. He sanctified Jesse and his sons, and called them to the sacrifice. When he beheld Eliab, the oldest, he was so impressed that he felt (in himself!) that "the Lord's anointed" had come before him first! But the Lord said to him:

"Look not on his countenance, or on the height of his stature; because I have refused him: for the Lord seeth not as man seeth; for man looketh on the outward appearance, but the Lord looketh on the heart" (16:7).

Perhaps Samuel felt a mild reproof. He may have thought of the height of Saul's stature; but what a disappointment! Then Samuel was inwardly reminded that he was only a "man," and his "eye judgment" was very limited. Only God's eyes could ponder the heart.

Finally all the sons there present had been refused, and the youngest one, the keeper of the sheep, was sent for. At last, a ruddy youth with a beautifully open countenance, and evidently "handsome," came in, and immediately the Lord said, *"Arise, anoint him: for this is he."*

When Samuel poured the anointing oil on the young man, "the Spirit of the Lord came upon David from that day forward." Fully satisfied in heart and soul, the aged prophet simply rose up and went home.

Some sixteen years passed before mention is made of Samuel again (1063 B.C.?). David was now an adult, fleeing for his life from a jealous-hearted King Saul, who was possessed with an evil spirit (19:18). After Saul's third attempt to kill his successor, David escaped and went to Samuel's home in Ramah. He told Samuel all that Saul had done to him. The aged prophet, though now possibly 107 years old, took David to "Naioth," which is said to have been one of Samuel's "schools of the prophets" in or near Ramah.

Saul heard where David was, and he sent men to capture him. Twice he did this, but when the messengers saw the "student prophets" and Samuel prophesying, they began prophesying also, and apparently were helpless to take David. Finally Saul himself went to Ramah, and the Lord took him into hand (19:22-24). And while he was in God's hand, David took his opportunity to move on.

If the chronology is accurate, *"Samuel died"* (25:1) in about 1060 B.C.—age 110 years. Saul lived perhaps four more years, constantly in pursuit of David, and plagued by the Philistines. He missed Samuel, for he could not get answers from the Lord himself. In utter desperation, he sought out the witch of Endor, who purportedly called forth the deceased Samuel, that he might inquire of him once more what to do in an impending battle with the Philistines (chapter 28). It was a prophecy of "gloom and doom"! Death for Saul and his sons, and a Philistine victory, would come "tomorrow"! (28:19) And it did! (About 1056 B.C.)

We join the writer of the *Epistle to the Hebrews,* who summarizes it well—

"And what shall I more say? for the time would fail me to tell of . . . Samuel, and of the prophets."

"And these all, having obtained a good report through faith, received not the promise:

"God having provided some better thing for us, that they without us should not be made perfect" (Hebrews 11:32, 39, 40).

God grant that we do not fail them!

FOR OUR ADMONITION AND LEARNING:

We should not despair when occasionally we seem to have "lost the way." God may be guiding us on an indirect route to some unexpected place where He wants us, and where He knows we would not go if He told us too much in advance. But thank God for men like Samuel, to whom He can send us for the counsel we need. What we find there may be far more important than what we *think* we are looking for.

Sometimes it becomes necessary to "make the best of a bad situation." Samuel filled the role well. The people had made a foolish request, but God had seen fit to grant them their wish. Samuel knew the Lord never makes a mistake. Regardless of the circumstances, the young king would need moral support. Samuel gave it as long as conscience would bear it. So should we in our own life situations.

Later on, when rebuke was in order, the aged prophet was still God's faithful messenger. Ministers of God will find it imperative to "crucify self" rather than make compromises, or evade responsibility. We must all give account of ourselves personally to God.

Someone has wisely said, *"They also serve who only stand and wait."* Samuel apparently experienced some waiting periods. James tells us, " . . . The trying of your faith worketh *patience.* But let patience have her perfect work, that ye may be perfect and entire, wanting nothing" (James 1:3, 4). Sometimes God needs somebody He can trust simply to "stand in the gap"

(Ezekiel 22:30), or "in the breach" (Psalms 106:23), pleading with Him to be merciful toward those who might otherwise be destroyed! In the first case, God could find none, so He poured out His indignation! In the second instance, Moses was able to turn God's wrath away from a people who were ill-deserving of mercy. "... Yea, many a time turned he his anger away, and did not stir up all his wrath" (Psalms 78:38). Who would say that those who thus "stand and wait" are not serving God's purpose?

THE JUDGES OF ISRAEL

Test Questions

1. There were _____ judges of Israel.
   (Twelve—Fifteen—Twenty-four—Fifty-three)

2. This course covers a period of about _____ years, according to the *Thompson Chain-Reference* chronology.
   (1000—1500—350—450—285—365)

3. The first of the judges was _____; the last was _____.

4. Israel dwelt in _____ during the *Period of the Judges*.
   (The wilderness—Babylon—Canaan—Assyria)

5. Write "True" or "False" before each of the following statements:
   (   ) All of the judges were good men.
   (   ) During this period "every man did that which was right in God's eyes."
   (   ) Gideon was judge during the first *Philistine Oppression*.
   (   ) Jephthah was the son of Gilead by a harlot.

6. Othniel and Ibzan were both from the tribe of _____.
   (Judah—Levi—Benjamin—Ephraim)

7. The two judges from the tribe of Levi were _____ and _____.
   (Jair—Deborah—Ehud—Eli—Elon—Gideon—Samuel—Samson)

8. Othniel delivered Israel from the _____ Oppression.
   (Philistine—Midianite—Mesopotamian—Ammonite)

9. Write the correct name in each blank:

   a. _____ was a very fat king.

   b. _____ slew the fat king.

c. _____ drove a tent pin through a man's head.

d. _____ was the man slain with the tent pin.

e. _____ was threshing wheat when God called him.

f. _____ was Gideon's other name.

g. _____ is said to have offered up his daughter as a burnt-offering.

h. _____ took a special interest in the marriages of his sixty children.

i. _____ slew more of the enemy in his death than in his life.

j. _____ was overly indulgent with his wicked sons.

10. Write "True" or "False" before each statement:

(   ) The *Period of the Judges* resulted from there being no one executive head appointed after Joshua's death.

(   ) Levi was mistaken in his judgment of Hannah as she prayed.

(   ) That Elon lived, judged, and died is all that is said about his ten-year reign.

(   ) Samuel was reared in the temple at Shiloh.

11. Fill the blanks with the proper names:

a. _____ had 40 sons and 30 nephews (grandsons) who rode on as many colts.

b. _____ went with Deborah to battle.

c. _____ slew his 70 half-brothers.

d. _____ was judge following the evil reign of Abimelech.

e. _____ was rejected by his half-brothers, who later called him home to be Israel's captain and judge.

12. a. The "tabernacle of the congregation" was located in the city of _____ by Joshua.
    (Bethel—Ramah—Shiloh—Gilgal)

    b. The "ark of the covenant" was taken by the _____ in battle.
    (Moabites—Ammonites—Philistines—Midianites)

    c. _____ was judge less than a year.
    (Elon—Abimelech—Abdon—Shamgar)

    d. _____ and _____ are said to have each judged Israel 80 years.
    (Othniel—Ehud—Jephthah—Samuel—Gideon)

13. Fill the blanks with the proper names:

    a. _____ was the judge who brought the *Canaanite Oppression* to an end.

    b. _____ slew 600 Philistines with an ox goad.

    c. _____ was the judge who anointed two kings.

    d. _____ delivered Israel out of the hands of the Midianites.

14. a. Abimelech destroyed the city of _____, where his mother's family lived.
    (Shiloh—Mizpeh—Shechem—Penuel—Aphek)
    b. Samuel's home city was _____.
    (Gibeah—Ramah—Shiloh—Kirjath-jearim)
    c. Saul and his family lived at _____.
    (Gilead—Gibeah—Timnath—Pirathon)
    d. Samson lived at _____.
    (Ramathaim-zeboim—Gilgal—Zorah—Etam)

15. Match by writing in the numbers from the second column before the names in the first column:
    (   ) a. Manoah   1. Father of Abimelech
    (   ) b. Elkanah   2. Father of Samuel
    (   ) c. Jesse   3. Father of Gideon
    (   ) d. Joash   4. Father of Samson

( ) e. Kenaz   5. Father of David
( ) f. Gideon   6. Father of Othniel

16. a. Caleb gave _____ his daughter Achsah for his wife.
    (Abdon—Ehud—Othniel—Shamgar—Ibzan)
    b. _____ was the left-handed judge.
    (Ehud—Jephthah—Abimelech—Elon—Othniel)
    c. Samson slew _____ men with the jawbone of an ass.
    (30—300—600—900—1,000—1,500)
    d. Sisera's Philistine army had _____ chariots of iron.
    (500—800—900—1,000)

17. _____ and _____ were Nazarites from birth.
    (Shamgar—Samson—Samuel—Gideon)

18. _____ and _____ were the sons of Samuel.
    (Hophni—Ebenezer—Joel—Abiah—Phinehas—Eleazer)

19. _____ and _____ were the sons of Eli.
    (Hophni—Belial—Ichabod—Phinehas—Eliab)

20. The nations which Israel did not drive out were left among them as _____ in their sides.
    (goads—swords—thorns—spears)

21. Put an X before each statement that applies:
    Samuel openly reproved King Saul for:
    a. ___ Taking upon himself a priestly duty.
    b. ___ Hiding among the stuff.
    c. ___ Disobedience in not utterly destroying the Amalekites.
    d. ___ Persecuting David.

22. Write "True" or "False" before each statement:
    (   ) The "ark of the covenant" was in Midianite hands seven months.
    (   ) The "ark" was in the house of Abinadab twenty years.
    (   ) Samuel filled three offices—judge, priest, and king.

23. Match by writing in the numbers from the second column before the names in the first column:
    (   ) a. Samuel   1. "Speak for thy servant heareth."
    (   ) b. Saul   2. "It is the Lord: let him do what seemeth him good."
    (   ) c. Eli   3. "Did ye not hate me, and expel me out of my father's house?"
    (   ) d. Samson   4. "Let me die with the Philistines."
    (   ) e. Jephthah 5. "I have sinned: yet honour me...."

24. Circle the right answers:
    a. Who visited a king in his summer parlor?
       (Eglon—Elon—Ehud—Eleazer)
    b. Who was called "a mother in Israel"?
       (Hannah—Peninnah—Deborah—Delilah)
    c. Who won a great battle with 300 men?
       (Gilead—Gideon—Gaal—Samson)
    d. Who perverted judgment by taking bribes?
       (Eli's sons—Saul—Samuel's sons—Jephthah's brethren)

25. Write "True" or "False" before each statement:
    (   ) Samson killed 300 foxes to settle the awards about the riddle.
    (   ) Jotham was the son of Gideon who likened the judge of Israel to a bramble.
    (   ) Tola "arose to defend Israel" following Abimelech's evil rule.
    (   ) Balak joined Deborah in song after the defeat of the Canaanites.

    NAME: _____

    ADDRESS: _____

    _____

NOTE: Please send all 25 questions in at the same time. PLEASE DO NOT SEND JUST A PORTION AT ANY ONE TIME. Thank you.

NOTES

NOTES